LENT DAILY MISSAL

Veritas

First published 1988 by
Veritas Publications
7-8 Lower Abbey Street
Dublin 1

Copyright © Veritas 1988

ISBN 1 85390 080 X

Extracts from the *Roman Missal, Lectionary,
Rite of Penance*
Concordat cum originali:
✠ Joseph Carroll
Dublin Diocesan Administrator

Additional material
cum permissu:
✠ Joseph Carroll
Dublin Diocesan Administrator

Cover design: Eddie McManus
Typesetting: Printset & Design Ltd, Dublin
Printed in the Republic of Ireland by
Mount Salus Press Ltd, Dublin

ACKNOWLEDGEMENTS

The text of the Order of Mass and Propers are copyright © International Committee on English in the Liturgy, Inc. All rights reserved.

The scripture texts are taken from *The Jerusalem Bible* copyright © 1966, 1967, 1968 Darton, Longman and Todd Ltd., and Doubleday & Co. Inc.

The version of the Psalms is copyright © The Grail (England) 1963, published by Collins in *The Psalms: A New Translation*, London, 1963. Acnowledgement is due to the International Committee on English Translation for the Gloria, Nicene Creed, Apostles' Creed, Sanctus and Dialogue before the Preface. The Propers for Ireland are copyright © the National Liturgical Commission.

The original Italian language edition of the *Stations of the Cross* by Pope John Paul II is copyright Libreria Editrice Vaticana, Italy.

CONTENTS

Introduction	1
The Order of Mass and the Proper Prefaces	3-20
Propers and Readings for weekdays during Lent	21-114
Proper of Saints	115-135
Penance Service	136
Stations of the Cross	141
Gloria and Creed	inside back cover

KEEPING LENT

Lent is a preparation for the celebration of Easter. For the Lenten liturgy disposes both catechumens and the faithful to celebrate the paschal mystery: catechumens, through the several stages of Christian initiation, the faithful, through reminders of their own baptism and through penitential practices.

(From: General Principles on the Liturgical Year, no. 27.)

To go to Mass during Lent has become a very popular way of keeping the season. It would be a mistake, though, to see celebrating Mass as a penitential exercise in itself. No doubt there are penitential aspects attached, such as giving up time for it or getting up earlier in the morning. Rather we should see taking part in the liturgy of Lent as a closer participation in the life of the Body of Christ. The liturgy is 'the primary and indispensable soure from which the faithful are to derive the true Christian spirit.' (*Liturgy Constitution, n. 14*)

In the Lenten liturgy we look at the human situation as we journey towards the celebration of the paschal mystery at Easter. We consider the struggles within us, we who are God's creation: the conflict between flesh and spirit, restlessness, unhappiness and sin, and the human need to be saved, redeemed, reconciled. From this comes the need for prayer and repentance: prayer that is based on hope in Christ as Saviour and Mediator, and repentance that expresses itself in Lenten fasting.

Going to Mass in Lent enables us to hear the Word of God proclaimed. This brings the message of repentance, but also proclaims faith, mercy, the means of rebirth and the meaning of baptism.

For the theme of baptism predominates in Lent — so many throughout the world are to be baptised at the Easter Vigil. 'To remember baptism means for us to remember that we are Christians, how we became Christians, and why we remain Christians.' (*Pope Paul VI*)

The liturgy of Lent centres on Christ, in his life among us as a man and in his saving mission. This culminates in his death and resurrection, which we celebrate in the Sacred Triduum, from Good Friday to Easter Sunday, the high point of the Church's life.

Keeping Lent

Going to Mass in Lent means more than just being there in the Church. It means a deeper consideration of the Holy Scriptures as they are put before us each day. It can lead us to other forms of prayer such as the Church's Morning and Evening Prayer, the Stations of the Cross, and the celebration of the Sacrament of Penance.

Above all it should bring us with the right dispositions to celebrate the Sacred Triduum, especially in the Easter Vigil. 'It will cast all of us under its salutary spell. That spell will free us from the many other spells cast on us by the senses and the world and will lead us to live in the reality of Christ.' *(Pope Paul VI)*

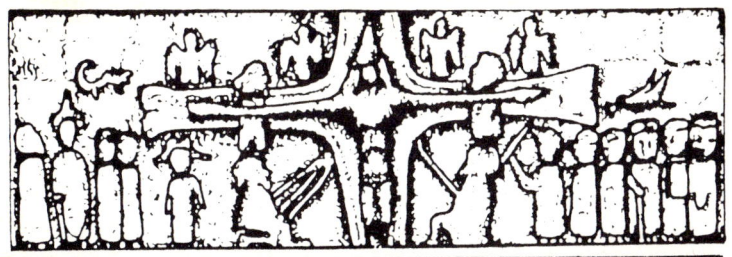

THE ORDER OF MASS

INTRODUCTORY RITES

The Greeting

When the song has ended, all make the sign of the cross with the priest:

P In the name of the Father, and of the Son, and of the Holy Spirit.

C Amen.

P The grace of our Lord Jesus Christ and the love of God and the fellowship of the Holy Spirit be with you all.

C And also with you.

or

P The grace and peace of God our Father and the Lord Jesus Christ be with you.

C Blessed be God, the Father of our Lord Jesus Christ.

or

C And also with you.

or

P The Lord be with you.

C And also with you.

After the greeting, the priest, or some other suitable minister, may give a brief introduction to the Mass of the day.

The rite of blessing and sprinkling holy water may be used as an alternative to the penitential rite.

Penitential Rite

The priest then invites the people to ask God to forgive their sins.

> My brothers and sisters,
> to prepare ourselves to celebrate
> the sacred mysteries, let us call to
> mind our sins.

First Form

All: **I confess to almighty God,
and to you, my brothers and
sisters, that I have sinned through
my own fault**
they strike their breast
**in my thoughts and in my words,
in what I have done,
and in what I have failed to do;**

and I ask blessed Mary, ever virgin, all the angels and saints, and you, my brothers and sisters, to pray for me to the Lord our God.

---

or second form

P Lord, we have sinned against you.
Lord, have mercy.

C **Lord, have mercy.**

P Lord, show us your mercy and love.

C **And grant us your salvation.**

---

or third form

P You were sent to heal the contrite:
Lord, have mercy.

C **Lord, have mercy.**

P You came to call sinners:
Christ, have mercy.

C **Christ, have mercy.**

P You plead for us at the right hand of the Father:
Lord, have mercy.

C **Lord, have mercy.**

The priest may use other versions of these forms.
Then the priest says the absolution.

P May almighty God have mercy on us, forgive us our sins, and bring us to everlasting life.

C **Amen.**

The Kyrie

The invocations, Lord, have mercy, *follow unless they have been used in one of the forms of the penitential rite.*

P Lord, have mercy.

C **Lord, have mercy.**

P Christ, have mercy.

C **Christ, have mercy.**

P Lord, have mercy.

C **Lord, have mercy.**

The Gloria

This prayer is said on Sundays, except during Advent and Lent, and on solemnities and feasts.

P Glory to God in the highest,

All: **and peace to his people on earth.**
Lord God, heavenly King,
almighty God and Father,
we worship you, we give you thanks,
we praise you for your glory.
Lord Jesus Christ, only Son of the Father,
Lord God, Lamb of God,
you take away the sin of the world:
have mercy on us;
you are seated at the right hand of the Father:
receive our prayer.
For you alone are the Holy One,
you alone are the Lord,
you alone are the Most High,
Jesus Christ,
with the Holy Spirit,
in the glory of God the Father.
Amen.

Opening Prayer

The priest now says the opening prayer, inviting the people with the words:

P Let us pray.

5 The Order of Mass

All pray quietly for a while. Then the priest says the proper prayer of the day. At the end the people answer: **Amen.**

LITURGY OF THE WORD

The texts of the Readings will be found under the day's Mass.

First Reading

At the end of the first reading the reader says: This is the Word of the Lord.

C **Thanks be to God.**

Responsorial Psalm

Second Reading

After the second reading the reader says: This is the Word of the Lord.

C **Thanks be to God.**

Gospel acclamation

The Alleluia then introduces the gospel reading. It may be omitted if not sung.

The Gospel

The priest or deacon who is to proclaim the gospel says: The Lord be with you.

C **And also with you.**
   A reading from the holy gospel according to N.

C **Glory to you, Lord.**

At the end of the gospel:
   This is the gospel of the Lord.

C **Praise to you, Lord Jesus Christ.**

The homily then follows and when it is ended all make the profession of faith.

Profession of Faith

P We believe in one God,

All: **the Father, the Almighty,**
maker of heaven and earth,
of all that is, seen and unseen.

We believe in one Lord,
   Jesus Christ,
the only Son of God,
eternally begotten of the Father,
God from God, Light from Light,
true God from true God,
begotten, not made,
of one Being with the Father.
Through him all things were
   made.
For us men and for our salvation
he came down from heaven:

all bow during these three lines:

by the power of the Holy Spirit
he became incarnate from the
Virgin Mary, and was made man.
For our sake he was crucified
under Pontius Pilate;
he suffered death and was
   buried.
On the third day he rose again
in accordance with the Scriptures;
he ascended into heaven
and is seated at the right hand of
the Father.

He will come again in glory to
judge the living and the dead,
and his kingdom will have no end.

We believe in the Holy Spirit, the
Lord, the giver of life,
who proceeds from the Father
and the Son.
With the Father and the Son

he is worshipped and glorified.
He has spoken through the Prophets.

We believe in one holy catholic and apostolic Church.

We acknowledge one baptism for the forgiveness of sins,

We look for the resurrection of the dead,

and the life of the world to come. Amen.

or

P I believe in God,
the Father almighty,
creator of heaven and earth.

All: **I believe in Jesus Christ, his only Son, our Lord.**

He was conceived by the power of the Holy Spirit and born of the Virgin Mary.

He suffered under Pontius Pilate, was crucified, died and was buried.

He descended to the dead.
On the third day he rose again.
He ascended into heaven, and is seated at the right hand of the Father.

He will come again to judge the living and the dead.

I believe in the Holy Spirit, the holy catholic Church, the communion of saints, the forgiveness of sins, the resurrection of the body, and life everlasting. Amen.

After each invocation the people respond:

C **Lord, graciously hear us.**
or similar words.

General Intercessions

The general intercessions (prayer of the faithful) conclude the liturgy of the word.

LITURGY OF THE EUCHARIST

An offertory song may be sung during the procession and the preparation of the gifts.

The priest takes the bread and says:

Blessed are you, Lord, God of all creation.
Through your goodness we have this bread to offer,
which earth has given and human hands have made.
It will become for us the bread of life.

If no offertory hymn is being sung the people reply:

Blessed be God for ever.

The priest then pours wine into the cup and adds a little water, saying quietly:

By the mystery of this water and wine may we come to share in the divinity of Christ, who humbled himself to share in our humanity.

He then takes the cup and says:

Blessed are you, Lord, God of all creation.
Through your goodness we have this wine to offer,
fruit of the vine and work of human hands.
It will become our spiritual drink.

If no offertory hymn is being sung the people again reply: **Blessed be God for ever.**

The priest then says quietly:
> Lord God, we ask you to receive us and be pleased with the sacrifice we offer you with humble and contrite hearts.

The priest now washes his fingers, saying quietly:
> Lord, wash away my iniquity; cleanse me from my sin.

Prayer over the Gifts
The priest invites the people to pray:

P Pray, brethren, that our sacrifice may be acceptable to God, the almighty Father.

C **May the Lord accept the sacrifice at your hands
for the praise and glory of his name,
for our good, and the good of all his Church.**

The priest then says the prayer over the gifts which concludes the preparation of the gifts and introduces the preparation of the eucharistic prayer. At the end of the prayer the people reply:

C **Amen.**

THE EUCHARISTIC PRAYER

The eucharistic prayer begins with the dialogue of the preface:

P The Lord be with you.

C **And also with you.**

P Lift up your hearts.

C **We lift them up to the Lord.**

P Let us give thanks to the Lord our God.

C **It is right to give him thanks and praise.**

> *The priest then says the preface of the day.*
> *At the end of the preface the people make their acclamation:*
> **Holy, holy, holy Lord, God of power and might,
> heaven and earth are full of your glory.
> > Hosanna in the highest.
> Blessed is he who comes in the name of the Lord.
> > Hosanna in the highest.**

PREFACES

PREFACE OF LENT I

Father, all-powerful and ever-living God, we do well always and everywhere to give you thanks through Jesus Christ our Lord.

Each year you give us this joyful season when we prepare to celebrate the paschal mystery with mind and heart renewed.
You give us a spirit of loving reverence for you, our Father, and of willing service to our neighbour.

As we recall the great events that gave us new life in Christ, you bring the image of your Son to perfection within us.

Now, with angels and archangels, and the whole company of heaven, we sing the unending hymn of your praise:
Holy, holy, holy. . .

PREFACE OF LENT II

Father, all-powerful and ever-living God, we do well always and everywhere to give you thanks.

This great season of grace is your gift to your family to renew us in spirit.

You give us strength to purify our hearts, to control our desires, and so to serve you in freedom. You teach us how to live in this passing world with our heart set on the world that will never end.

Now, with all the saints and angels, we praise you for ever:
Holy, holy, holy. . .

PREFACE OF LENT III

Father, all-powerful and ever-living God, we do well always and everywhere to give you thanks.

You ask us to express our thanks by self-denial.
We are to master our sinfulness and conquer our pride.
We are to show to those in need your goodness to ourselves.

Now, with all the saints and angels, we praise you for ever:
Holy, holy, holy. . .

PREFACE OF LENT IV

Father, all-powerful and ever-living God, we do well always and everywhere to give you thanks.

Through our observance of Lent you correct our faults and raise our minds to you, you help us grow in holiness, and offer us the reward of everlasting life through Jesus Christ our Lord.

Through him the angels and all the choirs of heaven worship in awe before your presence.

May our voices be one with theirs as they sing with joy the hymn of your glory:
Holy, holy, holy. . .

PREFACE OF THE PASSION OF THE LORD I

Father, all-powerful and ever-living God, we do well always and everywhere to give you thanks.

The suffering and death of your Son brought life to the whole world, moving our hearts to praise your glory. The power of the cross reveals your judgment on this world and the kingship of Christ crucified.

We praise you, Lord, with all the angels and saints in their song of joy:
Holy, holy, holy. . .

PREFACE OF THE PASSION OF THE LORD II

Father, all-powerful and ever-living God, we do well always and everywhere to give you thanks through Jesus Christ our Lord.

The days of his life-giving death and glorious resurrection are approaching. This is the hour when he triumphed over Satan's pride, the time when we celebrate the great event of our redemption.

Through Christ the angels of heaven offer their prayer of adoration as they rejoice in your presence for ever.
May our voices be one with theirs in their triumphant hymn of praise:
Holy, holy, holy. . .

EUCHARISTIC PRAYER I

or ROMAN CANON

We come to you, Father,
with praise and thanksgiving,
through Jesus Christ your Son.
Through him we ask you to accept
and bless ✠
these gifts we offer you in sacrifice.

We offer them for your holy catholic Church,
watch over it, Lord, and guide it;
grant it peace and unity throughout the world.

We offer them for *N.* our Pope,
for *N.* our bishop,
and for all who hold and teach the catholic faith
that comes to us from the apostles.

Remember, Lord, your people,
especially those for whom we now pray,
N. and *N.*
Remember all of us gathered here before you.
You know how firmly we believe in you
and dedicate ourselves to you.
We offer you this sacrifice of praise
for ourselves and those who are dear to us.
We pray to you, our living and true God,
for our well-being and redemption.

In union with the whole Church
we honour Mary, §
the ever-virgin mother of Jesus Christ our Lord and God.
We honour Joseph, her husband,
the apostles and martyrs
Peter and Paul, Andrew,

(James, John, Thomas,
James, Philip, Bartholomew, Matthew,
   Simon and Jude;
we honour Linus, Cletus, Clement,
Sixtus, Cornelius, Cyprian, Lawrence,
   Chrysogonus,
John and Paul, Cosmas and Damian)
and all the saints.
May their merits and prayers
gain us your constant help
   and protection.
(Through Christ our Lord. Amen.)

Bless and approve our offering;
make it acceptable to you,
an offering in spirit and in truth.
Let it become for us
the body and blood of Jesus Christ,
your only Son, our Lord.

The day before he suffered
(*Holy Thursday:* to save us and all men,
   that is today)
he took bread in his sacred hands
and looking up to heaven,
to you, his almighty Father,
he gave you thanks and praise.
He broke the bread,
gave it to his disciples, and said:
Take this, all of you, and eat it:
This is my body which will be given
   up for you.

When supper was ended
he took the cup.
Again he gave you thanks and praise,
gave the cup to his disciples, and said:

Take this, all of you, and drink from it:
this is the cup of my blood,
the blood of the new and everlasting
   covenant.
It will be shed for you and for all (men)
so that sins may be forgiven.
Do this in memory of me.

Acclamation of the people

P Let us proclaim the mystery of faith:

C **1 Christ has died,
   Christ is risen,
   Christ will come again.**

Alternative forms

**2 Dying you destroyed our death,
   rising you restored our life.
   Lord Jesus, come in glory.**

**3 When we eat this bread and
   drink this cup
   we proclaim your death, Lord
   Jesus,
   until you come in glory.**

**4 Lord, by your cross and
   resurrection
   you have set us free.
   You are the Saviour of the
   world.**

Father, we celebrate the memory of
   Christ, your Son.
We, your people and your ministers,
   recall his passion,
his resurrection from the dead,
and his ascension into glory;
and from the many gifts you have given
   us
we offer to you, God of glory and
   majesty,
this holy and perfect sacrifice:
the bread of life
and the cup of eternal salvation.

Look with favour on these offerings

and accept them as once you accepted
the gifts of your servant Abel,
the sacrifice of Abraham, our father in faith,
and the bread and wine offered by your priest Melchisedech.

Almighty God,
we pray that your angel may take this sacrifice
to your altar in heaven.
Then, as we receive from this altar
the sacred body and blood of your Son,
let us be filled with every grace and blessing.
(Through Christ our Lord. Amen.)

Remember, Lord, those who have died and have gone before us marked with the sign of faith, especially those for whom we now pray, N. and N.
May these, and all who sleep in Christ, find in your presence light, happiness, and peace.
(Through Christ our Lord. Amen.)

For ourselves, too, we ask some share in the fellowship of your apostles and martyrs, with John the Baptist, Stephen, Matthias, Barnabas, (Ignatius, Alexander, Marcellinus, Peter, Felicity, Perpetua, Agatha, Lucy, Agnes, Cecilia, Anastasia) and all the saints.
Though we are sinners,
we trust in your mercy and love.
Do not consider what we truly deserve,
but grant us your forgiveness.
Through Christ our Lord
you give us all these gifts.
You fill them with life and goodness,
you bless them and make them holy.

Through him,
with him,
in him,
in the unity of the Holy Spirit,
all glory and honour is yours,
almighty Father,
for ever and ever.

C Amen.

EUCHARISTIC PRAYER II

Preface
Other prefaces may be used in place of the following preface.
Father, it is our duty and our salvation, always and everywhere
to give you thanks
through your beloved Son, Jesus Christ.

He is the Word through whom you made the universe,
the Saviour you sent to redeem us.
By the power of the Holy Spirit
he took flesh and was born of the Virgin Mary.
For our sake he opened his arms on the cross;
he put an end to death
and revealed the resurrection.
In this he fulfilled your will
and won for you a holy people.

And so we join with the angels and saints
in proclaiming your glory
as we sing (say):

**Holy, holy, holy Lord, God of power and might,
heaven and earth are full of your glory.
Hosanna in the highest.**

**Blessed is he who comes in the name of the Lord.
Hosanna in the highest.**

Lord, you are holy indeed,
the fountain of all holiness.
Let your Spirit come upon these gifts to make them holy,
so that they may become for us
the body ✠ and blood of our Lord, Jesus Christ.

Before he was given up to death,
a death he freely accepted,
he took bread and gave you thanks.
He broke the bread,
gave it to his disciples, and said:

Take this, all of you, and eat it:
this is my body which will be given up for you.

When supper was ended, he took the cup.
Again he gave you thanks and praise,
gave the cup to his disciples, and said:

Take this, all of you, and drink from it:
this is the cup of my blood,
the blood of the new and everlasting covenant.
It will be shed for you and for all (men)
so that sins may be forgiven.
Do this in memory of me.

Acclamation of the people

P Let us proclaim the mystery of faith:

C 1 **Christ has died,
Christ is risen,
Christ will come again.**

Alternative forms

2 **Dying you destroyed our death,
rising you restored our life.
Lord Jesus, come in glory.**

3 **When we eat this bread and drink this cup
we proclaim your death, Lord Jesus,
until you come in glory.**

4 **Lord, by your cross and resurrection you have set us free.
You are the Saviour of the world.**

In memory of his death and resurrection, we offer you, Father, this life-giving bread, this saving cup.
We thank you for counting us worthy to stand in your presence and serve you.

May all of us who share in the body and blood of Christ be brought together in unity by the Holy Spirit.

Lord, remember your Church throughout the world;
make us grow in love,
together with N. our Pope,
N. our bishop, and all the clergy.

Prayer for the dead
Remember our brothers and sisters
who have gone to their rest
in the hope of rising again;
bring them and all the departed
into the light of your presence.

Have mercy on us all;
make us worthy to share eternal life
with Mary, the virgin Mother of God,
with the apostles, and with all the saints
who have done your will throughout the ages.
May we praise you in union with them,
and give you glory through your Son, Jesus Christ.

Through him,
with him,
in him,
in the unity of the Holy Spirit,
all glory and honour is yours,
almighty Father,
for ever and ever.

C **Amen.**

EUCHARISTIC PRAYER III

Father, you are holy indeed,
and all creation rightly gives you praise.
All life, all holiness comes from you
through your Son, Jesus Christ
   our Lord,
by the working of the Holy Spirit.
From age to age you gather a people to
   yourself,
so that from east to west
a perfect offering may be made
to the glory of your name.

And so, Father, we bring you these gifts.
We ask you to make them holy by the
   power of your Spirit,
that they may become the body ✠ and
   blood
of your Son, our Lord Jesus Christ,
at whose command we celebrate this
   eucharist.
On the night he was betrayed,
he took bread and gave you thanks and
   praise.
He broke the bread, gave it to his
   disciples, and said:
Take this, all of you, and eat it:
this is my body which will be given
   up for you.

When supper was ended,
he took the cup.
Again he gave you thanks and praise,
gave the cup to his disciples, and said:

Take this, all of you, and drink from it:
this is the cup of my blood,
the blood of the new and everlasting
   covenant.
It will be shed for you and for all
   men so that sins may be forgiven.
Do this in memory of me.

Acclamation of the people

P Let us proclaim the mystery of faith:

C **1 Christ has died,
Christ is risen,
Christ will come again.**

Alternative forms

**2 Dying you destroyed our death,
rising you restored our life.
Lord Jesus, come in glory.**

**3 When we eat this bread and
drink this cup
we proclaim your death, Lord
Jesus,
until you come in glory.**

**4 Lord, by your cross and
resurrection you have set us
free.
You are the Saviour of the
world.**

5 *for Ireland only* **My Lord and my
God.**

Father, calling to mind the death your
   Son endured for our salvation,
his glorious resurrection and ascension
   into heaven,

and ready to greet him when he comes again,
we offer you in thanksgiving this holy and living sacrifice.

Look with favour on your Church's offering, and see the Victim whose death has reconciled us to yourself.
Grant that we, who are nourished by his body and blood,
may be filled with his Holy Spirit,
and become one body, one spirit in Christ.

May he make us an everlasting gift to you
and enable us to share in the inheritance of your saints,
with Mary, the virgin Mother of God;
with the apostles, the martyrs,
(Saint N.: *the patron saint or the saint of the day*) and all your saints,
on whose constant intercession we rely for help.

Lord, may this sacrifice,
which has made our peace with you,
advance the peace and salvation of all the world.

Strengthen in faith and love your pilgrim Church on earth:
your servant, Pope N., our bishop N., and all the bishops,
with the clergy and the entire people your Son has gained for you.
Father, hear the prayers of the family you have gathered here before you.
In mercy and love unite all your children wherever they may be.

Welcome into your kingdom our departed brothers and sisters,
and all who have left this world in your friendship.

We hope to enjoy for ever the vision of your glory,
through Christ our Lord, from whom all good things come.

Through him,
with him,
in him,
in the unity of the Holy Spirit,
all glory and honour is yours,
almighty Father,
for ever and ever.

C **Amen.**

EUCHARISTIC PRAYER FOR MASSES OF RECONCILIATION I

The Lord be with you.
C **And also with you.**

Lift up your hearts.
C **We lift them up to the Lord.**

Let us give thanks to the Lord our God.
C **It is right to give him thanks and praise.**

Father, all-powerful and ever-living God, we do well always and everywhere to give you thanks and praise. You never cease to call us to a new and more abundant life.

God of love and mercy, you are always ready to forgive;
we are sinners,
and you invite us to trust in your mercy.

Time and time again we broke your covenant, but you did not abandon us. Instead, through your Son,
 Jesus our Lord,
you bound yourself even more closely

to the human family by a bond that can never be broken.

Now is the time
for your people to turn back to you
and to be renewed in Christ your Son,
a time of grace and reconciliation.

You invite us
to serve the family of mankind
by opening our hearts
to the fullness of your Holy Spirit.

In wonder and gratitude,
we join our voices with the choirs of heaven
to proclaim the power of your love
and to sing of our salvation in Christ:

All say:

Holy, holy, holy Lord,
   God of power and might,
heaven and earth are full of your glory.
Hosanna in the highest.
Blessed is he who comes in the name of the Lord.
Hosanna in the highest.

Father,
from the beginning of time
you have always done what is good for man
so that we may be holy as you are holy.

Look with kindness on your people gathered here before you:
send forth the power of your Spirit
so that these gifts may become for us
the body ✠ and blood of your beloved Son, Jesus the Christ,
in whom we have become your sons and daughters.

When we were lost
and could not find the way to you,
you loved us more than ever:

Jesus, your Son, innocent and without sin,
gave himself into our hands
and was nailed to the cross.
Yet before he stretched out his arms between heaven and earth
in the everlasting sign of your covenant,
he desired to celebrate the Paschal feast
in the company of his disciples.

While they were at supper
he took bread and gave you thanks and praise.
He broke the bread,
gave it to his disciples, and said:

Take this, all of you, and eat it:
This is my body which will be given up for you.

At the end of the meal,
knowing that he was to reconcile all things in himself
by the blood of his cross,
he took the cup, filled with wine.
Again he gave you thanks, handed the cup to his friends, and said:

Take this, all of you, and drink from it:
this is the cup of my blood,
the blood of the new and everlasting Covenant.
It will be shed for you and for all men
so that sins may be forgiven.
Do this in memory of me.

Acclamation of the people

P Let us proclaim the mystery of faith:

C **1 Christ has died,**
   Christ is risen,
   Christ will come again.

Alternative forms

   2 **Dying you destroyed our death,
     rising you restored our life.
     Lord Jesus, come in glory.**
   3 **When we eat this bread and
     drink this cup
     we proclaim your death, Lord
     Jesus,
     until you come in glory.**
   4 **Lord, by your cross and
     resurrection you have set us
     free.
     You are the Saviour of the
     world.**

We do this in memory of Jesus Christ,
our Passover and our lasting peace.
We celebrate his death and
   resurrection
and look for the coming of that day
when he will return to give us the
   fullness of joy.
Therefore we offer you, God ever
   faithful and true,
the sacrifice which restores man to your
   friendship.

Father,
look with love
on those you have called
to share in the one sacrifice of Christ.
By the power of your Holy Spirit
make them one body,
healed of all division.

Keep us all
in communion of mind and heart
with N., our Pope, N.,
   our bishop.
Help us to work together
for the coming of your kingdom,
until at last we stand in your presence
to share the life of the saints,
in the company of the Virgin Mary and
   the apostles,
and of our departed brothers and sisters
whom we commend to your memory.

Then, freed from every shadow of
   death,
we shall take our place in the new
   creation
and give you thanks
with Christ, our risen Lord.

Through him,
with him,
in him,
in the unity of the Holy Spirit,
all glory and honour is yours,
almighty Father,
for ever and ever.
C **Amen.**

EUCHARISTIC PRAYER FOR MASSES OF RECONCILIATION II

The Lord be with you.
C **And also with you.**

Lift up your hearts.
C **We lift them up to the Lord.**

Let us give thanks to the Lord our God.
C **It is right to give him thanks
     and praise.**

Father, all-powerful and ever-living
God, we praise and thank you through
   Jesus our Lord
for your presence and action in the
   world.

17 The Order of Mass

In the midst of conflict and division,
we know it is you
who turns our minds to thoughts of peace.
Your spirit changes our hearts:
enemies begin to speak to one another,
those who are estranged join hands in friendship,
and nations seek the way of peace together.

Your Spirit is at work
when understanding puts an end to strife, and vengeance gives way to forgiveness.
For this we should never cease
to thank and praise you.
We join with all the choirs of heaven
as they sing for ever to your glory:

All say:

> **Holy, holy, holy Lord,**
> **God of power and might,**
> **heaven and earth are full of your glory.**
> **Hosanna in the highest.**
> **Blessed is he who comes in the name of the Lord.**
> **Hosanna in the highest.**

God of power and might,
we praise you through your Son, Jesus Christ,
who comes in your name.
He is the Word that brings salvation.
He is the hand you stretch out to sinners.
He is the way that leads to your peace.

God our Father,
we had wandered far from you,
but through your Son you have brought us back.
You gave him up to death
so that we might turn again to you
and find our way to one another.

Therefore we celebrate the reconciliation Christ has gained for us.
We ask you to sanctify these gifts
by the power of your Spirit,
as we now fulfil your Son's
✠ command.

While he was at supper
on the night before he died for us,
he took bread in his hands,
and gave you thanks and praise.
He broke the bread,
gave it to his disciples, and said:

Take this, all of you, and eat it:
This is my body which will be given up for you.

At the end of the meal he took the cup.
Again he praised you for your goodness,
gave the cup to his disciples,
and said:

Take this, all of you, and drink from it:
this is the cup of my blood,
the blood of the new and everlasting Covenant.
It will be shed for you and for all men
so that sins may be forgiven.
Do this in memory of me.

Acclamation of the people

P Let us proclaim the mystery of faith:

C 1 **Christ has died,**
  Christ is risen,
  Christ will come again.

Alternative forms
  2 **Dying you destroyed our death,**
    rising you restored our life.

Lord Jesus, come in glory.

3 **When we eat this bread and drink this cup
we proclaim your death, Lord Jesus,
until you come in glory.**

4 **Lord, by your cross and resurrection you have set us free.
You are the Saviour of the world.**

5 *for Ireland only* **My Lord and my God.**

Lord our God,
your Son has entrusted to us
this pledge of his love.
We celebrate the memory of his death and resurrection
and bring you the gift you have given us, the sacrifice of reconciliation.
Therefore, we ask you, Father,
to accept us, together with your Son.

Fill us with his Spirit
through our sharing in this meal.
May he take away all that divides us.
May this Spirit keep us always in communion with N., our Pope, N., our bishop, (and his assistant bishops), with all the bishops and all your people.
Father, make your Church throughout the world
a sign of unity and an instrument of your peace.

You have gathered us here
around the table of your Son,
in fellowship with the Virgin Mary, Mother of God, and all the saints.
In that new world where the fullness of your peace will be revealed,
gather people of every race, language, and way of life
to share in the one eternal banquet
with Jesus Christ the Lord.

Through him,
with him,
in him,
in the unity of the Holy Spirit,
all glory and honour is yours,
almighty Father,
for ever and ever.

C Amen.

COMMUNION RITE

The Lord's Prayer

The priest introduces this prayer, using these or similar words:

P Let us pray with confidence to the Father in the words our Saviour gave us:

He continues, with the people:

**Our Father, who art in heaven,
hallowed be thy name.
Thy kingdom come.
Thy will be done on earth,
as it is in heaven.
Give us this day our daily bread,
and forgive us our trespasses,
as we forgive those
who trespass against us,
and lead us not into temptation,
but deliver us from evil.**

P Deliver us, Lord, from every evil, and grant us peace in our day.
In your mercy keep us free from sin and protect us from all anxiety as we wait in joyful hope for the coming of our Saviour, Jesus Christ.

C **For the kingdom, the power, and the glory are yours, now and for ever.**

P Lord Jesus Christ, you said to your apostles:
I leave you peace,
my peace I give you.
Look not on our sins, but on the faith of your Church, and grant us the peace and unity of your kingdom where you live for ever and ever.

C **Amen.**

P The peace of the Lord be with you always.

C **And also with you.**

The priest may add:

P Let us offer each other the sign of peace.

According to local custom, all offer each other a sign of peace and unity.

The priest takes the host and breaks it over the paten. He then puts a small fragment in the chalice. While he does this the people say or sing:

C **Lamb of God, you take away the sins of the world: have mercy on us.**

Lamb of God, you take away the sins of the world: have mercy on us.

Lamb of God, you take away the sins of the world: grant us peace.

Communion

The priest says one of the following prayers quietly:

P Lord Jesus Christ, Son of the living God, by the will of the Father and the work of the Holy Spirit your death brought life to the world. By your holy body and blood free me from all my sins and from every evil. Keep me faithful to your teaching, and never let me be parted from you.

---

or

P Lord Jesus Christ, with faith in your love and mercy I eat your body and drink your blood. Let it not bring me condemnation, but health in mind and body.

The priest then invites the people to communion:

P This is the Lamb of God who takes away the sins of the world.
Happy are those who are called to his supper.

Priest and people then say together:

Lord, I am not worthy to receive you, but only say the word and I shall be healed.

To each communicant the priest says:

P The body of Christ.

C **Amen.**

Prayer after Communion

P Let us pray.

At the end of the prayer the people reply: **Amen.**

Announcements to the congregation may be made at this time.

CONCLUDING RITE

Blessing and Dismissal

P The Lord be with you.

C **And also with you.**

P May almighty God bless you, the Father and the Son, ✠ and the Holy Spirit.

C **Amen.**

On certain days or occasions another more solemn form of blessing or prayer over the people may be used.

Solemn Blessing

P Bow your heads and ask for God's blessing.

5. *The Passion of the Lord*
The Father of mercies has given us an example of unselfish love in the sufferings of his only Son.
Through your service of God and neighbour may you receive his countless blessings.

C **Amen.**

You believe that by his dying Christ destroyed death for ever.
May he give you everlasting life.

C **Amen.**

He humbled himself for our sakes. May you follow his example and share in his resurrection.

C **Amen.**

May almighty God bless you, the Father, and the Son, ✠ and the Holy Spirit.

C **Amen.**

Prayers over the People

15. Lord,
have pity on your people;
help them each day to avoid what displeases you and grant that they may serve you with joy.
We ask this through Christ our Lord.

C **Amen.**

16. Father,
look with love upon your people, the love which our Lord Jesus Christ showed us when he delivered himself to evil men and suffered the agony of the cross, for he is Lord for ever.

C **Amen.**

18. Lord,
grant that your faithful people may continually desire to relive the mystery of the eucharist and so be reborn to lead a new life.
We ask this through Christ our Lord.

C **Amen.**

24. Father,
look kindly on your children who put their trust in you; bless them and keep them from all harm, strengthen them against the attacks of the devil.
May they never offend you but seek to love you in all they do.
We ask this through Christ our Lord.

C **Amen.**

The dismissal follows:

P The Mass is ended, go in peace.

C **Thanks be to God.**

Alternative forms

P Go in the peace of Christ.

C **Thanks be to God.**

or

P Go in peace to love and serve the Lord.

C **Thanks be to God.**

LITURGY OF THE WORD

ASH WEDNESDAY

This is the day of salvation.
Scripture reminds us today that our sign of the ashes is not to be an external thing only. God judges the heart of each of us, and knows our inner attitudes. The grace of God calls us to full reconciliation, a real change of heart.

Entrance Antiphon
Lord, you are merciful to all, and hate nothing you have created. You overlook the sins of men to bring them to repentance. You are the Lord our God.

The penitential rite and the Gloria are omitted.

Opening Prayer
Let us pray
  [for the grace to keep Lent faithfully]

Lord,
protect us in our struggle against evil.
As we begin the discipline of Lent,
make this season holy by our self-denial.

or

Let us pray
[in quiet remembrance of our need for redemption]

Father in heaven,
the light of your truth bestows sight
to the darkness of sinful eyes.
May this season of repentance
bring us the blessing of your forgiveness
and the gift of your light.

When the blessing and distribution of ashes is done apart from Mass these readings may be used for a liturgy of the word before the blessing of ashes.

Liturgy of the Word
First Reading

A reading from the prophet Joel.
2:12-18
Let your hearts be broken, not your garments torn.

'Now, now — it is the Lord who speaks —
come back to me with all your heart,
fasting, weeping, mourning.'
Let your hearts be broken not your garments torn,
turn to the Lord your God again,
for he is all tenderness and compassion,
slow to anger, rich in graciousness,
and ready to relent.
Who knows if he will not turn again, will not relent,
will not leave a blessing as he passes,

oblation and libation
for the Lord your God?
Sound the trumpet in Zion!
Order a fast,
proclaim a solemn assembly,
call the people together,
summon the community,
assemble the elders,
gather the children,
even the infants at the breast.
Let the bridegroom leave his bedroom
and the bride her alcove.
Between vestibule and altar let the priests,
the ministers of the Lord, lament.
Let them say,
"Spare your people, Lord!"
Do not make your heritage a thing of shame,
a byword for the nations.
Why should it be said among the nations,
"Where is their God?"'
Then the Lord, jealous on behalf of his land,
took pity on his people.

This is the word of the Lord.

Responsional Psalm Ps 50:3-6. 12-14. 17. v.3

Have mercy on us, O Lord, for we have sinned.

1 Have mercy on me, God, in your kindness.
   In your compassion blot out my offence.
   O wash me more and more from my guilt
   and cleanse me from my sin. ℟

2 My offences truly I know them;
   my sin is always before me.
   Against you, you alone, have I sinned:
   what is evil in your sight I have done. ℟

3 A pure heart create for me, O God,
   put a steadfast spirit within me.
   Do not cast me away from your presence,
   nor deprive me of your holy spirit. ℟

4 Give me again the joy of your help;
   with a spirit of fervour sustain me.
   O Lord, open my lips
   and my mouth shall declare your praise. ℟

Second Reading

A reading from the second letter of St Paul to the Corinthians   5:20 – 6:2
Be reconciled to God . . . now is the favourable time.

We are ambassadors for Christ; it is as though God were appealing through us, and the appeal that we make in Christ's name is: be reconciled to God. For our sake God made the sinless one into sin, so that in him we might become the goodness of God. As his fellow workers, we beg you once again not to neglect the grace of God that you have received. For he says: At the favourable time, I have listened to you; on the day of salvation I came to your help. Well, now is the favourable time; this is the day of salvation.

This is the word of the Lord.

Gospel Acclamation
                              Ps 50:12.14
Praise to you, O Christ, king of eternal glory!
A pure heart create for me, O God,
and give me again the joy of your help.
Praise to you, O Christ, king of eternal glory!

or   cf. Ps 94:8

Praise to you, O Christ, king of eternal glory!
Harden not your hearts today,
but listen to the voice of the Lord.
Praise to you, O Christ, king of eternal glory!

Gospel

A reading from the holy Gospel according to Matthew   6:1-6. 16-18
Your Father, who sees all that is done in secret, will reward you.

Jesus said to his disciples:
'Be careful not to parade your good deeds before men to attract their notice; by doing this you will lose all reward from your Father in heaven. So when you give alms, do not have it trumpeted before you; this is what the hypocrites do in the synagogues and in the streets to win men's admiration. I tell you solemnly, they have had their reward. But when you give alms, your left hand must not know what your right is doing; your almsgiving must be secret, and your Father who sees all that is done in secret will reward you.

'And when you pray, do not imitate the hypocrites: they love to say their prayers standing up in the synagogues and at the street corners for people to see them. I tell you solemnly, they have had their reward. But when you pray go to your private room and, when you have shut your door, pray to your Father who is in that secret place, and your Father who sees all that is done in secret will reward you.

'When you fast do not put on a gloomy look as the hypocrites do: they pull long faces to let men know they are fasting. I tell you solemnly, they have had their reward. But when you fast, put oil on your head and wash your face, so that no one will know you are fasting except your Father who see all that is done in secret; and your Father who sees all that is done in secret will reward you.'

This is the Gospel of the Lord.

Blessing and Giving of Ashes
After the homily the priest joins his hands and says:
Dear friends in Christ,
let us ask our Father

to bless these ashes
which we will use
as the mark of our repentance.

Silent prayer

Lord,
bless the sinner who asks for your forgiveness
and bless ✠ all those who receive these ashes.
May they keep this lenten season
in preparation for the joy of Easter.

or

Lord,
bless these ashes ✠
by which we show that we are dust.
Pardon our sins
and keep us faithful to the discipline of Lent,
for you do not want sinners to die
but to live with the risen Christ,
who reigns with you for ever and ever.

He sprinkles the ashes with holy water in silence.
The priest then places ashes on those who come forward, saying to each:

Turn away from sin and be faithful to the gospel.

or

Remember, man, you are dust and to dust you will return.

Meanwhile some of the following antiphons or other appropriate songs are sung.

1 Come back to the Lord with all your heart;
  leave the past in ashes,
  and turn to God with tears and fasting,
  for he is slow to anger and ready to forgive.

2 Let the priests and ministers of the Lord
  lament before his altar, and say:
  Spare us, Lord; spare your people!
  Do not let us die for we are crying out to you.

3 Lord, take away our wickedness.

Responsory
Direct our hearts to better things, O Lord;
heal our sin and ignorance.
Lord, do not face us suddenly with death,
but give us time to repent.

℟ **Turn to us with mercy, Lord; we have sinned against you.**
   Help us, God our saviour,
   rescue us for the honour of your name.
℟ **Turn to us with mercy, Lord; we have sinned against you.**

THURSDAY AFTER ASH WEDNESDAY

Let him take up his cross everyday. *The word of God puts a choice before us at the beginning of Lent: whether to live or die. God says: "I set before you life or death, blessing or curse." All our Lenten renunciation and self-sacrifice is not so much a dying as a striving after new life. Self seeking is death seeking.*

Entrance Antiphon
When I cry to the Lord, he hears my voice and saves me from the foes who threaten me. Unload your burden onto the Lord, and he will support you.

Opening Prayer
Lord,
may everything we do
begin with your inspiration,
continue with your help,
and reach perfection under your guidance.

Liturgy of the Word
First Reading

A reading from the book of Deuteronomy 30:15-20
See, I set before you today a blessing and a curse.

Moses said to the people: 'See, today I set before you life and prosperity, death and disaster. If you obey the commandments of the Lord your God that I enjoin on you today, if you love the Lord

After the giving of ashes the priest washes his hands; the rite concludes with the prayer of the faithful.
The Profession of Faith *is omitted.*

Prayer over the Gifts
Lord,
help us to resist temptation
by our lenten works of charity and penance.
By this sacrifice
may we be prepared to celebrate
the death and resurrection of Christ our Saviour
and be cleansed from sin and renewed in spirit.

Preface of Lent I-IV, p.8

Communion Antiphon
The man who meditates day and night on the law of the Lord will yield fruit in due season.

Prayer after Communion
Lord,
through this communion
may our lenten penance give you glory
and bring us your protection.

Solemn Blessing or Prayer over the People (p.20)

Thursday after Ash Wednesday

your God and follow his ways, if you keep his commandments, his laws, his customs, you will live and increase, and the Lord your God will bless you in the land which you are entering to make your own. But if your heart strays, if you refuse to listen, if you let yourself be drawn into worshipping other gods and serving them, I tell you today, you will most certainly perish; you will not live long in the land you are crossing the Jordan to enter and possess. I call heaven and earth to witness against you today: I set before you life or death, blessing or curse. Choose life, then, so that you and your descendants may live in the love of the Lord your God, obeying his voice, clinging to him; for in this your life consists, and on this depends your long stay in the land which the Lord swore to your fathers Abraham, Isaac and Jacob he would give them.'

This is the word of the Lord.

Responsorial Psalm
    Ps 1:1-4.6. ℟ *Ps 39:5*
℟ **Happy the man who has placed**
his trust in the Lord.

1 Happy indeed is the man
 who follows not the counsel
  of the wicked;
 nor lingers in the way of
  sinners
 nor sits in the company of
  scorners,
but whose delight is the law
 of the Lord,
and who ponders his law day
 and night. ℟

2 He is like a tree that is
  planted
 beside the flowing waters,
 that yields its fruit in due
  season
 and whose leaves shall never
  fade;
 and all that he does shall
  prosper. ℟

3 Not so are the wicked, not
  so!
 For they like winnowed chaff
 shall be driven away by the
  wind;
 for the Lord guards the way
  of the just
 but the way of the wicked
  leads to doom. ℟

Gospel Acclamation
      Ps 50:12.14
Praise and honour to you, Lord Jesus!
A pure heart create for me, O God,
and give me again the joy of your help.
Praise and honour to you, Lord Jesus!

or   *Mt 4:17*
Praise and honour to you, Lord Jesus!
Repent, says the Lord,
for the kingdom of heaven is close at hand.
Praise and honour to you, Lord Jesus!

Gospel

A reading from the holy Gospel according to Luke 9:22-25
Anyone who loses his life for my sake, that man will save it.

Jesus said to his disciples: 'The Son of Man is destined to suffer grievously, to be rejected by the elders and chief priests and scribes and to be put to death, and to be raised up on the third day.'

Then to all he said, 'If anyone wants to be a follower of mine, let him renounce himself and take up his cross every day and follow me. For anyone who wants to save his life will lose it; but anyone who loses his life for my sake, that man will save it. What gain, then, is it for a man to have won the whole world and to have lost or ruined his very self?'

This is the Gospel of the Lord.

Prayer over the Gifts
Lord,
accept these gifts.
May they bring us your mercy and give you honour and praise.

Preface of Lent I-IV, p.8.

Communion Antiphon: Create a clean heart in me, O God; give me a new and steadfast spirit.

Prayer after Communion
Merciful Father,
may the gifts and blessings we receive
bring us pardon and salvation.

Solemn Blessing or Prayer over the People (p.20)

FRIDAY AFTER ASH WEDNESDAY

Is not this the sort of fast that pleases me? *Fasting is a very old religious tradition and should not be neglected, even though fasting from food is not imposed by obligation any longer. Fasting shows our dependence on God, our need for him. It helps us to discipline our unruly passions, and expresses our desire to support those who are in real need. It should not be too difficult to discover what each one needs to fast from.*

Entrance Antiphon
The Lord heard me and took pity on me. He came to my help.

Opening Prayer
Lord,
with your loving care
guide the penance we have begun.
Help us to persevere with love and sincerity.

Liturgy of the Word
First Reading

A reading from the prophet Isaiah 58:1-9
Is not this the sort of fast that pleases me?

Friday after Ash Wednesday

Thus says the Lord:
> Shout for all you are worth,
> raise your voice like a trumpet.
> Proclaim their faults to my people,
> their sins to the House of Jacob.
>
> They seek me day after day,
> they long to know my ways,
> like a nation that wants to act with integrity
> and not ignore the law of its God.
>
> They ask me for laws that are just,
> they long for god to draw near:
> 'Why should we fast if you never see it,
> why do penance if you never notice?'
>
> Look, you do business on your fastdays,
> you oppress all your workmen;
> look, you quarrel and squabble when you fast
> and strike the poor man with your fist.
>
> Fasting like yours today
> will never make your voice heard on high.
> Is that the sort of fast that pleases me,
> a truly penitential day for men?
>
> Hanging your head like a reed,
> lying down on sackcloth and ashes?
> Is that what you call fasting,
> a day acceptable to the Lord?
>
> Is not this the sort of fast that pleases me
> — it is the Lord who speaks —
>
> to break unjust fetters
> and undo the thongs of the yoke,
> to let the oppressed go free,
> and break every yoke,
> to share your bread with the hungry,
> and shelter the homeless poor,
> to clothe the man you see to be naked
> and not turn from your own kin?
> Then will your light shine like the dawn
> and your wound be quickly healed over.
>
> Your integrity will go before you
> and the glory of the Lord behind you.
> Cry, and the Lord will answer;
> call, and he will say, 'I am here.'

This is the word of the Lord.

Responsorial Psalm   Ps 50:3-6. 18-19. ℟ v. 19

℟ **A humbled, contrite heart, O God, you will not spurn.**

29 Friday after Ash Wednesday

1. Have mercy on me, God, in your kindness.
   In your compassion blot out my offence.
   O wash me more and more from my guilt
   and cleanse me from my sin. ℟

2. My offences truly I know them,
   my sin is always before me.
   Against you, you alone, have I sinned;
   what is evil in your sight I have done. ℟

3. For in sacrifice you take no delight,
   burnt offering from me you would refuse,
   my sacrifice a contrite spirit.
   A humbled, contrite heart you will not spurn. ℟

Gospel Acclamation
                cf. Ps 129:5. 7

Glory and praise to you, O Christ!
My soul is waiting for the Lord,
I count on his word,
because with the Lord there is mercy
and fullness of redemption.
Glory and praise to you, O Christ!

or   cf. Amos 5:14

Glory and praise to you, O Christ!
Seek good and not evil so that you may live,
and that the Lord God of hosts may really be with you.
Glory and praise to you, O Christ!

Gospel

A reading from the holy Gospel according to Matthew   9:14-15
When the bridegroom is taken from them, then they will fast.

John's disciples came to Jesus and said, 'Why is it that we and the Pharisees fast, but your disciples do not?' Jesus replied, 'Surely the bridegroom's attendants would never think of mourning as long as the bridegroom is still with them? But the time will come for the bridegroom to be taken away from them, and then they will fast.'

This is the Gospel of the Lord.

Prayer over the Gifts
Lord,
through this lenten eucharist
may we grow in your love and service
and become an acceptable offering to you.

Preface of Lent I-IV, p.8.

Communion Antiphon
Teach us your ways, O Lord,
and lead us in your paths.

Prayer after Communion
Lord,
may our sharing in this mystery
free us from our sins

SATURDAY AFTER ASH WEDNESDAY

I have come to call sinners to repentance. *How should we live during Lent? The readings tell us to be concerned about people, especially those in need, to rejoice in the worship of God especially on the Lord's Day, and to follow Jesus with confidence knowing that as sinners he cares for us.*

Entrance Antiphon
Answer us, Lord, with your loving-kindness, turn to us in your great mercy.

Opening Prayer
Father,
look upon our weakness
and reach out to help us with your loving power.

Liturgy of the Word
First Reading

A reading from the prophet Isaiah   58:9-14
Your light will rise in the darkness.

The Lord says this:
    If you do away with the yoke,
    the clenched first, the wicked word,
if you give your bread to the hungry,
and relief to the oppressed,
your light will rise in the darkness,
and your shadows become like noon.
The Lord will always guide you,
giving you relief in desert places.
He will give strength to your bones
and you shall be like a watered garden,
like a spring of water
whose waters never run dry.
You will rebuild the ancient ruins,
build up on the old foundations.
You will be called 'Breach-mender',
'Restorer of ruined houses'.
If you refrain from trampling the sabbath,
and doing business on the holy day,
if you call the sabbath 'Delightful',
and the day sacred to the Lord 'Honourable',
if you honour it by abstaining from travel,
from doing business and from gossip,
then you shall find happiness in the Lord
and I will lead you triumphant over the heights of the land.
I will feed you on the

Saturday after Ash Wednesday

heritage of Jacob your
father.
For the mouth of the Lord
has spoken.

This is the word of the Lord.

Responsorial Psalm   Ps 85:1-6.
℟ v. 11

℟ **Show me, Lord, your way so that I may walk in your truth.**

1 Turn your ear, O Lord, and give answer
for I am poor and needy.
Preserve my life, for I am faithful:
save the servant who trusts in you. ℟

2 You are my God, have mercy on me, Lord,
for I cry to you all the day long.
Give joy to your servant, O Lord,
for to you I lift up my soul. ℟

3 O Lord, you are good and forgiving,
full of love to all who call,
Give heed, O Lord, to my prayer
and attend to the sound of my voice. ℟

Gospel Acclamation   cf. Ps 94:8
Glory to you, O Christ, you are the Word of God!
Harden not your hearts today,
but listen to the voice of the Lord.
Glory to you, O Christ, you are the Word of God!

or   Ez 33:11

Glory to you, O Christ, you are the Word of God!
I take pleasure, not in the death of a wicked man —
it is the Lord who speaks —
but in the turning back of a wicked man
who changes his ways to win life.
Glory to you, O Christ, you are the Word of God!

Gospel

A reading from the holy Gospel according to Luke   5:27-32

I have not come to call the virtuous, but sinners to repentance.

Jesus noticed a tax collector, Levi by name, sitting by the customs house, and said to him, 'Follow me.' And leaving everything he got up and followed him.

In his honour Levi held a great reception in his house, and with them at table was a large gathering of tax collectors and others. The Pharisees and their scribes complained to his disciples and said, 'Why do you eat and drink with tax collectors and sinners?' Jesus said to them in reply, 'It is not those who are well who need the doctor, but the sick. I have not come to call the virtuous, but sinners to repentance.'

This is the Gospel of the Lord.

Prayer over the Gifts
Lord,
receive our sacrifice of praise and reconciliation.
Let it free us from sin
and enable us to give you loving service.

Preface of Lent I-IV, p.8.

Communion Antiphon: It is mercy that I want, and not sacrifice, says the Lord; I did not come to call the virtuous, but sinners.

Prayer after Communion
Lord,
we are nourished by the bread of life you give us.
May this mystery we now celebrate help us to reach eternal life with you.

Solemn Blessing or Prayer over the People (p.20)

FIRST WEEK OF LENT
MONDAY

In so far as you did this to one of the least . . . you did it to me.
Living Lent, and indeed living our Christian lives, is not about external observances only. Again today we are reminded that we must love others from the heart. If we want to find Jesus we have to look for him in the world, in the people we meet daily. A Christian community is a sharing one.

Entrance Antiphon
As the eyes of servants are on the hands of their master, so our eyes are fixed on the Lord our God, pleading for his mercy. Have mercy on us, Lord, have mercy.

Opening Prayer
God our Saviour,
bring us back to you
and fill our minds with your wisdom.
May we be enriched by our observance of Lent.

Liturgy of the Word
First Reading

A reading from the book of Leviticus   19:1-2.11-18
You must pass judgement on your neighbour according to justice.

The Lord spoke to Moses; he said: 'Speak to the whole community of the sons of Israel and say to them: "Be holy, for I, the Lord your God, am holy.

"You must not steal nor deal deceitfully or fraudulently with your neighbour. You must not swear false by my name, profaning the name of your God. I am the Lord. You must not exploit or rob your neighbour. You must not keep back the labourer's wage until next morning. You must not curse the dumb, nor put an obstacle in the blind man's way, but you must fear your God. I am the Lord.

"You must not be guilty of unjust verdicts. You must neither be partial to the little man nor overawed by the great; you must pass judgement on your neighbour according to justice. You must not slander your own people, and you must not jeopardise your neighbour's life. I am the Lord. You must not bear hatred for your brother in your heart. You must openly tell him, your neighbour, of his offence; this way you will not take a sin upon yourself. You must not exact vengeance, nor must you bear a grudge against the children of your people. You must love your neighbour as yourself. I am the Lord.'"

This is the word of the Lord.

Responsorial Psalm
     Ps 18:8-10, 15. ℟ Jn 6:64
℟ **Your words are spirit, Lord, and they are life.**

1 The law of the Lord is perfect,
 it revives the soul.
 The rule of the Lord is to be trusted,
 it gives wisdom to the simple. ℟

2 The precepts of the Lord are right,
 they gladden the heart.
 The command of the Lord is clear,
 it gives light to the eyes. ℟

3 The fear of the Lord is holy, abiding for ever.
 The decrees of the Lord are truth
 and all of them just. ℟

4 May the spoken words of my mouth,
 the thoughts of my heart,
 win favour in your sight, O Lord,
 my rescuer, my rock! ℟

Gospel Acclamation   Ez 18:31
 Praise to you, O Christ, king of eternal glory!
 Shake off all your sins — it is the Lord who speaks —
 and make yourselves a new heart and a new spirit.
 Praise to you, O Christ, king of eternal glory!

or   2 Cor 6:2

 Praise to you, O Christ, king of eternal glory!
 Now is the favourable time;
 this is the day of salvation.
 Praise to you, O Christ, king of eternal glory!

Gospel

A reading from the holy Gospel according to Matthew   25:31-46
In so far as you did this to one of the least of these brothers of mine you did it to me.

Jesus said to his disciples: 'When the Son of Man comes in his glory, escorted by all the angels, then he will take his seat on his throne of glory. All the nations will be assembled before him and he will separate men one from another as the shepherd separates sheep from goats. He will place the sheep on his right hand and the goats on his left. Then the King will say to those on his right hand, "Come, you whom my Father has blessed, take for your heritage the kingdom prepared for you since the foundation of the world. For I was hungry and you gave me food; I was thirsty and you gave me drink; I was a stranger and you made me welcome; naked and you clothed me, sick and you visited me, in prison and you came to see me." Then the virtuous will say to him in reply, "Lord, when did we see you hungry and feed you; or thirsty and give you drink? When did we see you a stranger and make you welcome; naked and clothe you; sick or in prison and go to see you?" And the King will answer, "I tell you solemnly, in so far as you did this to one of the least of these brothers of mine, you did it to me". Next he will say to those on his left hand, "Go away from me, with your curse upon you, to the eternal fire prepared for the devil and his angels. For I was hungry and you never gave me food; I was thirsty and you never gave me anything to drink; I was a stranger and you never made me welcome, naked and you never clothed me, sick and in prison and you never visited me." Then it will be their turn to ask, "Lord, when did we see you hungry or thirsty, a stranger or naked, sick or in prison, and did not come to your help?" Then he will answer, "I tell you solemnly, in so far as you neglected to do this to one of the least of these, you neglected to do it to me." And they will go away to eternal punishment, and the virtuous to eternal life.'

This is the Gospel of the Lord.

Prayer over the Gifts
Lord,
may this offering of our love
be acceptable to you.
Let it transform our lives
and bring us your mercy.

Preface of Lent I-IV, p.8.

Communion Antiphon
I tell you, anything you did for the least of my brothers, you did for me, says the Lord. Come, you whom my Father has blessed; inherit the kingdom prepared for you since the foundation of the world.

Prayer after Communion
Lord,
through this sacrament
may we rejoice in your healing power
and experience your saving love in mind and body.

Solemn Blessing or Prayer over the People (p.20)

TUESDAY

My word shall succeed in what it was sent to do. *We should have*

First Week of Lent: Tuesday

great trust in the power of prayer. The prayer that Jesus gives us is one that is powerful, for it is the word of God and does not return empty. But it must be prayed with sentiments of contrition and reconciliation.

Entrance Antiphon
In every age, O Lord, you have been our refuge. From all eternity, you are God.

Opening Prayer
Father,
Look on us, your children.
Through the discipline of Lent help us to grow in our desire for you.

Liturgy of the Word
First reading

A reading from the prophet Isaiah
55:10-11
My word shall succeed in what it was sent to do.

Thus says the Lord:
 As the rain and the snow come down from the heavens and do not return without watering the earth, making it yield and giving growth to provide seed for the sower and bread for the eating, so the word that goes from my mouth does not return to me empty, without carrying out my will and succeeding in what it was sent to do.

This is the word of the Lord.

Responsorial Psalm   Ps 33:4-7, 16-19. ℟ v.18
℟ **The Lord rescues the just in all their distress.**

1 Glorify the Lord with me.
  Together let us praise his name.
  I sought the Lord and he answered me;
  from all my terrors he set me free. ℟

2 Look towards him and be radiant;
  let your faces not be abashed.
  This poor man called; the Lord heard him
  and rescued him from all his distress. ℟

3 The Lord turns his face against the wicked
  to destroy their remembrance from the earth.
  The Lord turns his eyes to the just
  and his ears to their appeal. ℟

4 They call and the Lord hears
  and rescues them in all their distress.
  The Lord is close to the broken-hearted;
  those whose spirit is crushed he will save. ℟

Gospel Acclamation   Mt 4:4
 Praise and honour to you, Lord Jesus!
 Man does not live on bread alone,

but on every word that
comes from the mouth of
God.
Praise and honour to you,
Lord Jesus!

Gospel

A reading from the holy Gospel according to Matthew 6:7-15
You should pray like this.

Jesus said to his disciples: 'In your prayers do not babble as the pagans do, for they think that by using many words they will make themselves heard. Do not be like them; your Father knows what you need before you ask him. So you should pray like this:

'Our Father in heaven,
may your name be held
holy,
your kingdom come,
your will be done,
on earth as in heaven.
Give us today our daily
bread.
And forgive us our debts,
as we have forgiven those
who are in debt to us.
And do not put us to the
test,
but save us from the evil
one.

'Yes, if you forgive others their failings, your heavenly Father will forgive you yours; but if you do not forgive others, your Father will not forgive your failings either.'

This is the Gospel of the Lord.

Prayer over the Gifts
Father of creation,
from all you have given us
we bring you this bread and wine.
May it become for us the food of
eternal life.

Preface of Lent I-IV. p.8.

Communion Antiphon: My God of justice, you answer my cry; you come to my help when I am in trouble. Take pity on me, Lord, and hear my prayer.

Prayer after Communion
Lord,
may we who receive this
sacrament
restrain our earthly desires
and grow in love for the things of
heaven.

*Solemn Blessing or Prayer over the
People* (p.20)

WEDNESDAY

When Jonah preached they repented. *We are called to repentance at this time. We must pray for the humbled, contrite heart. It is not necessarily those who have heard God's message and seem to have accepted it who are truly converted. It is a great step forward to be able to acknowledge the need for conversion.*

Entrance Antiphon
Remember your mercies, Lord, your tenderness from ages past. Do

not let our enemies triumph over us; O God, deliver Israel from all her distress.

Opening Prayer
Lord,
look upon us and hear our prayer.
By the good works you inspire help us to discipline our bodies and to be renewed in spirit.

Liturgy of the Word
First reading

A reading from the prophet Jonah
                                    3:1-10
The people of Nineveh renounced their evil behaviour.

The word of the Lord was addressed to Jonah: 'Up!' he said, 'Go to Nineveh, the great city, and preach to them as I told you to.' Jonah set out and went to Nineveh in obedience to the word of the Lord. Now Nineveh was a city great beyond compare: it took three days to cross it. Jonah went on into the city, making a day's journey. He preached in these words, 'Only forty days more and Nineveh is going to be destroyed.' And the people of Nineveh believed in God; they proclaimed a fast and put on sackcloth, from the greatest to the least. The news reached the king of Nineveh, who rose from his throne, took off his robe, put on sackcloth and sat down in ashes. A proclamation was then promulgated throughout Nineveh, by decree of the king and his ministers, as follows: 'Men and beasts, herds and flocks, are to taste nothing; they must not eat, they must not drink water. All are to put on sackcloth and call on God with all their might; and let everyone renounce his evil behaviour and the wicked things he has done. Who knows if God will not change his mind and relent, if he will not renounce his burning wrath, so that we do not perish? God saw their efforts to renounce their evil behaviour. And God relented: he did not inflict on them the disaster which he had threatened.

This is the word of the Lord.

Responsorial Psalm   Ps 50:3-4,
                            12-13, 18-19. ℟ v.19
℟ **A humbled, contrite heart, O God, you will not spurn.**

1 Have mercy on me, God, in
    your kindness.
  In your compassion blot out
    my offence.
  O wash me more and more
    from my guilt
  and cleanse me from my sin.
    ℟

2 A pure heart create for me,
    O God,
  put a steadfast spirit within
    me.
  Do not cast me away from
    your presence,
  nor deprive me of your holy
    spirit. ℟

3 For in sacrifice you take no
    delight,
  burnt offering from me you
    would refuse,

my sacrifice a contrite spirit.
A humbled, contrite heart
   you will not spurn. ℟

Gospel Acclamation   *Ez 33:11*
Glory and praise to you,
O Christ!
I take pleasure, not in the
   death of a wicked man —
it is the Lord who speaks —
who in the turning back of a
   wicked man
who changes his ways to win
   life.
Glory and praise to you,
O Christ!

or   *Joel 2:12-13*

Glory and praise to you,
O Christ!
Now, now — it is the Lord
   who speaks —
come back to me with all
   your heart,
for I am all tenderness and
   compassion.
Glory and praise to you,
O Christ!

Gospel

A reading from the holy Gospel according to Luke   11:29-32
The only sign given to this generation is the sign of Jonah.

The crowds got even bigger and Jesus addressed them. 'This is a wicked generation; it is asking for a sign. The only sign it will be given is the sign of Jonah. For just as Jonah became a sign to the Ninevites, so will the Son of Man be to this generation. On Judgement day the Queen of the South will rise up with the men of this generation and condemn them, because she came from the ends of the earth to hear the wisdom of Solomon; and there is something greater than Solomon here. On Judgement day the men of Nineveh will stand up with this generation and condemn it, because when Jonah preached they repented; and there is something greater than Jonah here.'

This is the Gospel of the Lord.

Prayer over the Gifts
Lord,
from all you have given us,
we bring you these gifts in your
   honour.
Make them the sacrament of our
   salvation.

Preface of Lent I-IV. p.8.

Communion Antiphon
Lord, give joy to all who trust in you; be their defender and make them happy for ever.

Prayer after Communion
Father,
you never fail to give us the food
   of life.
May this eucharist renew our
   strength
and bring us to salvation.

*Solemn Blessing or Prayer over the
   People* (p.20)

THURSDAY

Ask, and it will be given to you.
Esther's prayer is that of one in great need, but it expresses the confidence that God will not abandon his own people. Jesus tells us that confident prayer will always be answered by our loving Father.

Entrance Antiphon
Let my words reach your ears, Lord; listen to my groaning, and hear the cry of my prayer, O my King, my God.

Opening Prayer
Father,
without you we can do nothing.
By your Spirit help us to know what is right
and to be eager in doing your will.

Liturgy of the Word
First Reading

A reading from the book of Esther 4:17
I have no helper but you, Lord.

Queen Esther took refuge with the Lord in the mortal peril which had overtaken her. She besought the Lord God of Israel in these words:

'My Lord, our King, the only one,
come to my help, for I am alone
and have no helper but you
and am about to take my life in my hands.

'I have been taught from my earliest years, in the bosom of my family, that you, Lord, chose Israel out of all the nations and our ancestors out of all the people of old times to be your heritage for ever; and that you have treated them as you promised. Remember, Lord; reveal yourself
in the time of our distress.

'As for me, give me courage, King of gods and master of all power.
Put persuasive words into my mouth
when I face the lion;
change his feeling into hatred for our enemy,
that the latter and all like him may be brought to their end.

'As for ourselves, save us by your hand,
and come to my help, for I am alone
and have no one but you, Lord.'

This is the word of the Lord.

Responsorial Psalm
Ps 137:1-3, 7-8. ℟ v.3
℟ **On the day I called, you answered me, O Lord.**

1 I thank you, Lord, with all my heart,
   you have heard the words of my mouth.
   Before the angels I will bless you.

1st Week of Lent: Thursday

I will adore before your holy temple. ℟

2 I thank you for your faithfulness and love
which excel all we ever knew of you.
On the day I called, you answered;
you increased the strength of my soul. ℟

3 You stretch out your hand and save me,
your hand will do all things for me.
Your love, O Lord, is eternal,
discard not the work of your hands. ℟

Gospel Acclamation Joel 2:12-13
Glory to you, O Christ, you are the Word of God!
Now, now — it is the Lord who speaks —
come back to me with all your heart,
for I am all tenderness and compassion.
Glory to you, O Christ, you are the Word of God!

or Ps 50:12. 14

Glory to you, O Christ, you are the Word of God!
A pure heart create for me, O God,
and give me again the joy of your help.
Glory to you, O Christ, you are the Word of God!

Gospel

A reading from the holy Gospel according to Matthew 7:7-12
The one who asks always receives.

Jesus said to his disciples: 'Ask, and it will be given to you; search, and you will find; knock, and the door will be opened to you. For the one who asks always receives; the one who searches always finds; the one who knocks will always have the door opened to him. Is there a man among you who would hand his son a stone when he asked for bread? Or would hand him a snake when he asked for a fish? If you, then, who are evil, know how to give your children what is good, how much more will your Father in heaven give good things to those who ask him!

'So always treat others as you would like them to treat you; that is the meaning of the Law and the Prophets.'

This is the Gospel of the Lord.

Prayer over the Gifts
Lord,
be close to your people,
accept our prayers and offerings,
and let us turn to you with all our hearts.

Preface of Lent I-IV p.8.

Communion Antiphon: Everyone who asks will receive; whoever seeks shall find, and to him who knocks it shall be opened.

Prayer after Communion
Lord our God,
renew us by these mysteries.
May they heal us now
and bring us eternal salvation.

Solemn Blessing or Prayer over the People (p.20)

FRIDAY

With the Lord there is mercy and fullness of redemption. *We must accept the consequences of our own wrongdoing. That personal responsibility will lead us to acknowledge our offence before God and seek forgiveness. And with the Lord there is mercy and full redemption. God's mercy is to be seen in the way we ourselves show mercy to others.*

Entrance Antiphon
Lord, deliver me from my distress.
See my hardship and my poverty,
and pardon all my sins.

Opening Prayer
Lord,
may our observance of Lent
help to renew us and prepare us
to celebrate the death and resurrection of Christ,
who lives and reigns. . . .

Liturgy of the Word
First Reading

A reading from the prophet Ezekiel
18:21-28

Am I likely to take pleasure in the death of a wicked man and not prefer to see him renounce his wickedness and live?
Thus says the Lord:

If the wicked man renounces all the sins he has committed, respects my laws and is law-abiding and honest, he will certainly live; he will not die. All the sins he committed will be forgotten from then on; he shall live because of the integrity he has practised. What! Am I likely to take pleasure in the death of a wicked man — it is the Lord who speaks — and not prefer to see him renounce his wickedness and live?

'But if the upright man renounces his integrity, commits sin, copies the wicked man and practises every kind of filth, is he to live? All the integrity he has practised shall be forgotten from then on, but this is because he himself has broken faith and committed sin, and for this he shall die. But you object, "What the Lord does is unjust." Listen, you House of Israel: is what I do unjust? Is it not what you do that is unjust? When the upright man renounces his integrity to commit sin and dies because of this, he dies because of the evil that he himself has committed. When the sinner renounces sin to become law-abiding and honest, he deserves to live. He has chosen to renounce all his previous sins, he shall certainly live; he shall not die.'

This is the word of the Lord.

First Week of Lent: Friday

Responsorial Psalm

Ps 129. ℟ v.3

℟ **If you, O Lord, should mark our guilt,
Lord, who would survive?**

1 Out of the depths I cry to you, O Lord,
Lord, hear my voice!
O let your ears be attentive
to the voice of my pleading. ℟

2 If you, O Lord, should mark our guilt,
Lord, who would survive?
But with you is found forgiveness:
for this we revere you. ℟

3 My soul is waiting for the Lord,
I count on his word.
My soul is longing for the Lord
more than watchman for daybreak.
Let the watchman count on daybreak
and Israel on the Lord. ℟

4 Because with the Lord there is mercy
and fullness of redemption,
Israel indeed he will redeem
from all its iniquity. ℟

Gospel Acclamation

cf. Amos 5:14

Praise to you, O Christ, king of eternal glory!
Seek good and not evil so that you may live,
and that the Lord God of hosts may really be with you.
Praise to you, O Christ, king of eternal glory!

or Ez 18:31

Praise to you, O Christ, king of eternal glory!
Shake off all your sins — it is the Lord who speaks —
and make yourselves a new heart and a new spirit.
Praise to you, O Christ, king of eternal glory!

Gospel

A reading from the holy Gospel according to Matthew 5:20-26

Go and be reconciled with your brother first.

Jesus said to his disciples: 'If your virtue goes no deeper than that of the scribes and Pharisees, you will never get into the kingdom of heaven.

'You have learnt how it was said to our ancestors: You must not kill, and if anyone does kill he must answer for it before the court. But I say this to you: anyone who is angry with his brother will answer for it before the court; if a man calls his brother "Fool" he will answer for it before the Sanhedrin, and if a man calls him "Renegade" he will answer for it in hell fire. So then, if you are bringing your offering to the altar and there remember that your brother has something against you, leave your offering there before the altar, go and be reconciled with your brother first, and then come back and present your offering. Come to terms with your opponent in good time while you are still on the way to the court with him, or he may hand you over to the judge and the judge to the officer, and you will be thrown into prison. I tell you solemnly, you will not get out till you have paid the last penny.'

This is the Gospel of the Lord.

Prayer over the Gifts
Lord of mercy,
in your love accept these gifts.
May they bring us your saving power.

Preface of Lent I-IV p.8.

Communion Antiphon
By my life, I do not wish the sinner to die, says the Lord, but to turn to me and live.

Prayer after Communion
Lord,
may the sacrament you give us
free us from our sinful ways and bring us new life.
May this eucharist lead us to salvation.

Solemn Blessing or Prayer over the People (p.20)

SATURDAY

Be perfect as your heavenly Father is perfect. *At the end of this first week of Lent we are to recall that through Baptism we are God's holy nation, a special people. By the covenant God wants us to observe faithfully all his commands, to live a life of love. Jesus describes that life as one of God's own perfection.*

Entrance Antiphon
The law of the Lord is perfect, reviving the soul; his commandments are the wisdom of the simple.

Opening Prayer
Eternal Father,
turn our hearts to you.
By seeking your kingdom
and loving one another,
may we become a people who worship you
in spirit and truth.

Liturgy of the Word
First Reading

A reading from the book of Deuteronomy 26:16-19
You will be a people consecrated to the Lord God.

Moses said to the people: 'The Lord your God today commands you to observe these laws and customs; you must keep and observe them with all your heart and with all your soul.

'You have today made this declaration about the Lord; that he will be your God, but only if you follow his ways, keep his statutes, his commandments, his ordinances, and listen to his voice. And the Lord has today made this declaration about you: that you will be his very own people as he promised you, but only if you keep all his commandments; then for praise and renown and honour he will set you high above all the nations he has made, and you will be a people consecrated to the Lord, as he promised.'

This is the word of the Lord.

Responsorial Psalm
  Ps 118:1-2, 4-5, 7-8. ℟ v.1
℟ **They are happy who follow God's law!**

1 They are happy whose life is blameless,
   who follow God's law!
   They are happy those who do his will,
   seeking him with all their hearts. ℟

2 You have laid down your precepts
   to be obeyed with care.
   May my footsteps be firm
   to obey your statutes. ℟

3 I will thank you with an upright heart
   as I learn your decrees.
   I will obey your statutes;
   do not forsake me. ℟

Gospel Acclamation   cf. Lk 8:15
   Praise and honour to you, Lord Jesus!
   Blessed are those who, with a noble and generous heart,
   take the word of God to themselves
   and yield a harvest through their perseverance.
   Praise and honour to you, Lord Jesus!

or   2 Cor 6:2

   Praise and honour to you, Lord Jesus!
   Now is the favourable time;
   this is the day of salvation.
   Praise and honour to you, Lord Jesus!

Gospel

A reading from the holy Gospel according to Matthew   5:43-48
Be perfect as your heavenly Father is perfect.
Jesus said to his disciples: 'You have learnt how it was said: You must love your neighbour and hate your enemy. But I say this to you: love your enemies and pray for those who persecute you; in this way you will be sons of your Father in heaven, for he causes the sun to rise on bad men as well as good, and his rain to fall on honest and dishonest men alike. For if you love those who love you, what right have you to claim any credit? Even the tax collectors do as much, do they not? And if you save your greetings for your brothers, are you doing anything exceptional? Even the pagans do as much, do they not? You must therefore be perfect just as your heavenly Father is perfect.'

This is the Gospel of the Lord.

Prayer over the Gifts
Lord,
may we be renewed by this eucharist.
May we become more like Christ your Son,
who is Lord for ever and ever.

Preface of Lent I-IV p.8.

Communion Antiphon: Be perfect, as your heavenly Father is perfect, says the Lord.

Prayer after Communion
Lord,
may the word we share
be our guide to peace in your kingdom.
May the food we receive
assure us of your constant love.

Solemn Blessing or Prayer over the People (p.20)

SECOND WEEK OF LENT

MONDAY

Do not judge and you will not be judged yourselves. *Daniel's prayer recalls God's greatness and his covenant with his people. It acknowledges that we should love God by obeying his commands, but also confesses failure. In our shame all we can do is throw ourselves on God's mercy. We will receive that mercy if we ourselves show it to others.*

Entrance Antiphon
Redeem me, Lord, and have mercy on me; my foot is set on the right path, I worship you in the great assembly.

Opening Prayer
God our Father,
teach us to find new life through penance.
Keep us from sin,
and help us live by your commandment of love.

Liturgy of the Word
First Reading

A reading from the prophet Daniel
9:4-10
We have sinned, we have done wrong.

O Lord, God great and to be feared, you keep the convenant and have kindness for those who love you and keep your commandments: we have sinned, we have done wrong, we have acted wickedly, we have betrayed your commandments and your ordinances and turned away from them. We have not listened to your servants the prophets, who spoke in your name to our kings, our princes, our ancestors, and to all the people of the land. Integrity, Lord, is yours; ours the look of shame we wear today, we, the people of Judah, the citizens of Jerusalem, the whole of Israel, near and far away, in every country to which you have dispersed us because of the treason we have committed against you. To us, Lord, the look of shame belongs, to our kings, our princes, our ancestors, because we have sinned against you. To the Lord our God mercy and pardon belong, because we have betrayed him, and have not listened to the voice of the Lord our God nor followed the laws he has given us through his servants the prophets.

This is the word of the Lord.

Responsorial Psalm
   Ps 78:8-9.11.13. ℟ *Ps 102:10*
℟ **Do not treat us according to our sins, O Lord.**

1 Do not hold the guilt of our fathers against us.
  Let your compassion hasten to meet us
  for we are in the depths of distress. ℟

2 O God our saviour, come to our help,
  come for the sake of the glory of your name.
  O Lord our God, forgive us our sins;
  rescue us for the sake of your name. ℟

3 Let the groans of the prisoners come before you;
  let your strong arm reprieve those condemned to die.
  But we, your people, the flock of your pasture,
  will give you thanks for ever and ever.
  We will tell your praise from age to age. ℟

Gospel Acclamation
   Praise and honour to you, Lord Jesus!
   The seed is the word of God, Christ the sower,
   whoever finds this seed will remain for ever.
   Praise and honour to you, Lord Jesus!

or   cf. *Jn 6:63, 68*

   Praise and honour to you, Lord Jesus!
   Your words are spirit, Lord and they are life;
   you have the message of eternal life.
   Praise and honour to you, Lord Jesus!

Gospel

A reading from the holy Gospel according to Luke   6:36-38
Grant pardon, and you will be pardoned.

Jesus said to his disciples: 'Be compassionate as your Father is compassionate. Do not judge, and you will not be judged yourselves; do not condemn, and you will not be condemned yourselves; grant pardon, and you will be pardoned. Give, and there will be gifts for you: a full measure, pressed down, shaken together, and running over, will be poured into your lap;

because the amount you measure out is the amount you will be given back.'

This is the Gospel of the Lord.

Prayer over the Gifts
Father of mercy,
hear our prayer.
May the grace of this mystery prevent us from becoming absorbed in material things.

Preface of Lent I-IV p.8.

Communion Antiphon
Be merciful as your Father is merciful, says the Lord.

Prayer after Communion
Lord,
may this communion bring us pardon
and lead us to the joy of heaven.

Solemn Blessing or Prayer over the People (p.20)

TUESDAY

Cease to do evil: learn to do good.
We are told today what God is looking for in each one of his people. God judges the innermost heart, the real intentions of our external actions. We have to be humble before him, compassionate to all, and practise what we preach.

Entrance Antiphon
Give light to my eyes, Lord, lest I sleep in death, and my enemy say: I have overcome him.

Opening Prayer
Lord,
watch over your Church,
and guide it with your unfailing love.
Protect us from what could harm us
and lead us to what will save us.
Help us always,
for without you we are bound to fail.

Liturgy of the Word
First Reading

A reading from the prophet Isaiah   1:10, 16-20
Learn to do good, search for justice.

Hear the word of the Lord,
you rulers of Sodom,
listen to the command of our God,
you people of Gomorrah.

   'Wash, make yourselves clean.
Take your wrong-doing out of my sight.

   'Cease to do evil.
Learn to do good,
search for justice,
help the oppressed,
be just to the orphan,
plead for the widow.

   'Come now, let us talk this over,
says the Lord.
Though your sins are like scarlet,

they shall be as white as
   snow;
though they are red as
   crimson,
they shall be like wool.

'If you are willing to obey,
you shall eat the good things
   of the earth.
But if you persist in rebellion,
the sword shall eat you
   instead.'
The mouth of the Lord has
   spoken.

This is the word of the Lord.

Responsorial Psalm   Ps 49:8-9. 16-17. 21. 23. ℟ v.23

℟ **I will show God's salvation to the upright.**

1 'I find no fault with your
      sacrifices,
   your offerings are always
      before me.
   I do not ask more bullocks
      from your farms,
   nor goats from among your
      herds. ℟

2 'But how can you recite my
      commandments
   and take my covenant on
      your lips,
   you who despise my law
   and throw my words to the
      winds. ℟

3 'You do this, and should I
      keep silence?
   Do you think that I am like
      you?
   A sacrifice of thanksgiving
      honours me
   and I will show God's
      salvation to the upright.'
   ℟

Gospel Acclamation   Mt 4:17
   Glory and praise to you,
      O Christ!
   Repent, says the Lord, for the
      kingdom of heaven is
      close at hand.
   Glory and praise to you,
      O Christ!

or   Ez 18:31

   Glory and praise to you,
      O Christ!
   Shake off all your sins — it is
      the Lord who speaks —
   and make yourselves a new
      heart and a new spirit.
   Glory and praise to you,
      O Christ!

Gospel

A reading from the holy Gospel according to Matthew   23:1-12
They do not practise what they preach.

Addressing the people and his disciples Jesus said, 'The scribes and the Pharisees occupy the chair of Moses. You must therefore do what they tell you and listen to what they say; but do not be guided by what they do, since they do not practise what they preach. They tie up heavy burdens and lay them on men's shoulders, but will they lift a finger to move them? Not they! Everything they do is done to attract attention, like wearing broader phylacteries and longer tassels, like wanting to take the place of honour at banquets and the front seats in the synagogues, being greeted obsequiously in the market squares and having people calling them Rabbi.

'You, however, must not allow yourselves to be called Rabbi, since you have only one Master, and you are all brothers. You must call no one on earth your father, since you have only one Father, and he is in heaven. Nor must you allow yourselves to be called teachers, for you have only one Teacher, the Christ. The greatest among you must be your servant. Anyone who exalts himself will be humbled and anyone who humbles himself will be exalted.'

This is the Gospel of the Lord.

Prayer over the Gifts
Lord,
bring us closer to you by this celebration.
May it cleanse us from our faults
and lead us to the gifts of heaven.

Preface of Lent I-IV p.8.

Communion Antiphon: I will tell all your marvellous works. I will rejoice and be glad in you, and sing to your name, Most High.

Prayer after Communion
Lord,
may the food we receive bring us your constant assistance
that we may live better lives.

Solemn Blessing or Prayer over the People (p.20)

WEDNESDAY

They will condemn him to death, to be mocked and scourged and crucified. *The privilege and dignity of following Christ should not blind us to the painful reality of service. All who follow Christ must, like him, seek to be the servants of all, and not look for positions of power. Jeremiah knew that doing God's work would bring him opposition and persecution. It brought death on the cross for Jesus.*

Entrance Antiphon
Do not abandon me, Lord, My God, do not go away from me! Hurry to help me, Lord, my Saviour.

Opening Prayer
Father,
teach us to live good lives,
encourage us with your support
and bring us to eternal life.

Liturgy of the Word
First Reading

A reading from the prophet Jeremiah   18:18-20
Come on, let us hit at him.

'Come on,' they said, 'let us concoct a plot against Jeremiah;

the priest will not run short of instruction without him, nor the sage of advice, nor the prophet of the word. Come on, let us hit at him with his own tongue; let us listen carefully to every word he says.'

Listen to me Lord,
hear what my adversaries are saying.
Should evil be returned for good?
For they are digging a pit for me.
Remember how I stood in your presence
to plead on their behalf,
to turn your wrath away from them.

This is the word of the Lord.

Responsorial Psalm   Ps 30:5-6, 14-16. ℟ v.17

℟ **Save me in your love, O Lord.**

1 Release me from the snares they have hidden
  for you are my refuge, Lord.
  Into your hands I commend my spirit.
  It is you who will redeem me, Lord. ℟

2 I have heard the slander of the crowd,
  fear is all around me,
  as they plot together against me,
  as they plan to take my life. ℟

3 But as for me, I trust in you, Lord,
  I say: 'You are my God.
  My life is in your hands, deliver me
  from the hands of those who hate me.'

℟ **Save me in your love, O Lord.**

Gospel Acclamation
                              cf. Jn 6:63, 68
Glory to you, O Christ, you are the Word of God!
Yours words are spirit, Lord, and they are life;
you have the message of eternal life.
Glory to you, O Christ, you are the word of God!

or   Jn 8:12

Glory to you, O Christ, you are the Word of God!
I am the light of the world, says the Lord;
anyone who follows me will have the light of life.
Glory to you, O Christ, you are the Word of God!

Gospel

A reading from the holy Gospel according to Matthew   20:17-28
They will condemn him to death.

Jesus was going up to Jerusalem, and on the way he took the Twelve to one side and said to them, 'Now we are going up to Jerusalem, and the Son of Man is about to be handed over to the chief priests and scribes. They will condemn him to death and will hand him over to the pagans to be mocked and scourged and crucified; and on the third day he will rise again.'

Then the mother of Zebedee's sons came with her sons to make a request of him, and bowed low; and he said to her, 'What is it you want?' She said to him, 'Promise that these two sons of mine may sit one at your right hand and the other at your left in your kingdom.' 'You do not know what you are asking,' Jesus answered. 'Can you drink the cup that I am going to drink?' They replied, 'We can.' 'Very well,' he said, 'you shall drink my cup, but as for seats at my right hand and my left, these are not mine to grant; they belong to those to whom they have been allotted by my Father.'

When the other ten heard this they were indignant with the two brothers. But Jesus called them to him and said, 'You know that among the pagans the rulers lord it over them, and their great men make their authority felt. This is not to happen among you. No; anyone who wants to be great among you must be your servant, and anyone who wants to be first among you must be your slave, just as the Son of Man came not to be served but to serve, and to give his life as a ransom for many.'

This is the Gospel of the Lord.

Prayer over the Gifts
Lord,
accept this sacrifice,
and through this holy exchange of gifts
free us from the sins that enslave us.

Preface of Lent I-IV p.8.

Communion Antiphon
The Son of Man did not come to be served, but to serve, and to give his life as a ransom for many.

Prayer after Communion
Lord our God,
may the eucharist you give us
as a pledge of unending life
help us to salvation.

Solemn Blessing or Prayer over the People (p.20)

THURSDAY

A blessing on the man who puts his trust in the Lord. *We can put our trust in material things to the extent that we end up with a heart that is "like dry scrub in the wastelands". The rich man did not do anything wrong to Lazarus, he failed by omission, by not opening his heart to the wretched beggar's condition.*

Entrance Antiphon
Test me, O God, and know my thoughts; see whether I step in the wrong path, and guide me along the everlasting way.

Opening Prayer
God of love,
bring us back to you.

Send your Spirit to make us strong in faith
and active in good works.

Liturgy of the Word
First Reading

A reading from the prophet Jeremiah 17:5-10

A curse on the man who puts his trust in man, a blessing on the man who puts his trust in the Lord.

The Lord says this:
'A curse on the man who puts his trust in man,
who relies on things of flesh,
whose heart turns from the Lord.

He is like dry scrub in the wastelands:
if good comes, he has no eyes for it,
he settles in the parched places of the wilderness,
a salt land, uninhabited.

'A blessing on the man who puts his trust in the Lord,
with the Lord for his hope.
He is like a tree by the waterside
that thrusts its roots to the stream:
when the heat comes it feels no alarm,
its foliage stays green;
it has no worries in a year of drought,
and never ceases to bear fruit.

'The heart is more devious than any other thing,
perverse too: who can pierce its secrets?
I, the Lord, search the heart,
I probe the loins
to give each man what his conduct
and actions deserve.'

This is the word of the Lord.

Responsorial Psalm Ps 1:1-4, 6.
℟ Ps. 39:5

℟ **Happy the man who has placed
his trust in the Lord.**

1 Happy indeed is the man
who follows not the counsel of the wicked;
nor lingers in the way of sinners
nor sits in the company of scorners,
but whose delight is the law of the Lord
and who ponders his law day and night. ℟

2 He is like a tree that is planted
beside the flowing waters
that yields its fruit in due season
and whose leaves shall never fade;
and all that he does shall prosper. ℟

3 Not so are the wicked, not so!
For they like winnowed chaff
shall be driven away by the wind.

Second Week of Lent: Thursday

For the Lord guards the way
of the just
but the way of the wicked
leads to doom. ℟

Gospel Acclamation   Lk 15:18
Praise to you, O Christ, king
of eternal glory!
I will leave this place and go
to my father and say:
'Father, I have sinned against
heaven and against you.'
Praise to you, O Christ, king
of eternal glory!

or   cf. Lk 8:15

Praise to you, O Christ, king
of eternal glory!
Blessed are those who, with
a noble and generous
heart,
take the word of God to
themselves
and yield a harvest through
their perseverance.
Praise to you, O Christ, king
of eternal glory!

Gospel

A reading from the holy Gospel according to Luke   16:19-31
Good things came your way, just as bad things came the way of Lazarus. Now he is being comforted here while you are in agony.

Jesus said to the Pharisees: 'There was a rich man who used to dress in purple and fine linen and feast magnificently every day. And at his gate there lay a poor man called Lazarus, covered with sores, who longed to fill himself with the scraps that fell from the rich man's table. Dogs even came and licked his sores. Now the poor man died and was carried away by the angels to the bosom of Abraham. The rich man also died and was buried.

'In his torment in Hades he looked up and saw Abraham a long way off with Lazarus in his bosom. So he cried out, "Father Abraham, pity me and send Lazarus to dip the tip of his finger in water and cool my tongue, for I am in agony in these flames." "My son", Abraham replied, "remember that during your life good things came your way, just as bad things came the way of Lazarus. Now he is being comforted here while you are in agony. But that is not all: between us and you a great gulf has been fixed, to stop anyone, if he wanted to, crossing from our side to yours, and to stop any crossing from your side to ours."

'The rich man replied, "Father, I beg you then to send Lazarus to my father's house, since I have five brothers, to give them warning so that they do not come to this place of torment too." "They have Moses and the prophets," said Abraham, "let them listen to them." "Ah no, father Abraham," said the rich man, "but if someone comes to them from the dead, they will repent." Then Abraham said to him, "If they will not listen either to Moses or to the prophets, they will not be convinced even if someone should rise from the dead."'

This is the Gospel of the Lord.

Prayer over the Gifts
Lord,
may this sacrifice bless our lenten observance.
May it lead us to sincere repentance.

Preface of Lent I-IV p.8.

Communion Antiphon
Happy are those of blameless life, who follow the law of the Lord.

Prayer after Communion
Lord,
may the sacrifice we have offered strengthen our faith
and be seen in our love for one another.

Solemn Blessing or Prayer over the People (p.20)

FRIDAY

The kingdom will be taken from you and given to those who will produce fruit. *The story of God's relationship with his people is one of a Father who loved them. He sent many tokens of his love through the prophets who were often rejected. At last he sent his son, and he was treated as those before him. If we do not accept Jesus and produce fruit we also will lose the kingdom.*

Entrance Antiphon
To you, Lord, I look for protection, never let me be disgraced. You are my refuge; save me from the trap they have laid for me.

Opening Prayer
Merciful Father,
may our acts of penance bring us your forgiveness,
open our hearts to your love,
and prepare us for the coming feast of the resurrection.

Liturgy of the Word
First Reading

A reading from the book of Genesis   37:3-4, 12-13, 17-28
Here comes the man of dreams. Come on, let us kill him.

Israel loved Joseph more than all his other sons, for he was the son of his old age, and he had a coat with long sleeves made for him. But his brothers, seeing how his father loved him more than all his other sons, came to hate him so much that they could not say a civil word to him.

His brothers went to pasture their father's flock at Shechem. Then Israel said to Joseph, 'Are not your brothers with the flock at Shechem? Come, I am going to send you to them.' So Joseph went after his brothers and found them at Dothan.

They saw him in the distance, and before he reached them they made a plot among themselves to put him to death. 'Here comes the man of dreams' they said to one another. 'Come on, let us kill him and throw him into some well; we can say that a wild beast devoured him. They we shall see what becomes of his dreams.'

But Reuben heard, and he saved him from their violence. 'We must not take his life,' he said. 'Shed no blood,' said Reuben to them, 'throw him into this well in the wilderness, but do not lay violent hands on him' — intending to save him from them and to restore him to his father. So, when Joseph reached his brothers, they pulled off his coat, the coat with long sleeves that he was wearing, and catching hold of him they threw him into the well, an empty well with no water in it. They then sat down to eat.

Looking up they saw a group of Ishmaelites who were coming from Gilead, their camels laden with gum, tragacanth, balsam and resin, which they were taking down into Egypt. Then Judah said to his brothers, 'What do we gain by killing our brother and covering up his blood? Come, let us sell him to the Ishmaelites, but let us not do any harm to him. After all, he is our brother, and our own flesh.' His brothers agreed.

Now some Midianite merchants were passing, and they drew Joseph up out of the well. They sold Joseph to the Ishmaelites for twenty silver pieces, and these men took Joseph to Egypt.

This is the word of the Lord.

Responsorial Psalm
Ps 104:16-21. ℟ v.5
℟ **Remember the wonders the Lord has done.**

1 God called down a famine on the land;
  he broke the staff that supported them.
  He had sent a man before them,
  Joseph, sold as a slave. ℟

2 His feet were put in chains,
  his neck was bound with iron,
  until what he said came to pass
  and the Lord's word proved him true. ℟

3 Then the king sent and released him;
  the ruler of the peoples set him free,
  making him master of his house
  and ruler of all he possessed. ℟

Gospel Acclamation   Jn 3:16
  Praise and honour to you, Lord Jesus!
  God loved the world so much that he gave his only Son;
  everyone who believes in him has eternal life.
  Praise and honour to you, Lord Jesus!

Gospel
A reading from the holy Gospel according to Matthew
21:22-34.45-46

This is the heir. Come on, let us kill him.

Jesus said to the chief priests and the elders of the people: 'Listen to another parable. There was a man, a landowner, who planted a vineyard; he fenced it round, dug a winepress in it and built a tower; then he leased it to tenants and went abroad. When vintage time drew near he sent his servants to the tenants to collect his produce. But the tenants seized his servants, thrashed one, killed another and stoned a third. Next he sent some more servants, this time a larger number, and they dealt with them in the same way. Finally he sent his son to them. "They will respect my son," he said. But when the tenants saw the son, they said to each other, "This is the heir. Come on, let us kill him and take over his inheritance." So they seized him and threw him out of the vineyard and killed him. Now when the owner of the vineyard comes, what will he do to those tenants?' They answered, 'He will bring those wretches to a wretched end and lease the vineyard to other tenants who will deliver the produce to him when the season arrives.' Jesus said to them, 'Have you never read in the scriptures:

> It was the stone rejected by the builders
> that became the keystone.
> This was the Lord's doing
> and it is wonderful to see?

'I tell you, then, that the kingdom of God will be taken from you and given to a people who will produce its fruit.'

When they heard his parables, the chief priests and the scribes realised he was speaking about them, but though they would have liked to arrest him they were afraid of the crowds, who looked on him as a prophet.

This is the Gospel of the Lord.

Prayer over the Gifts
God of mercy,
prepare us to celebrate these
 mysteries.
Help us to live the love they
 proclaim.

Preface of Lent I-IV p.8.

Communion Antiphon
God loved us and sent his Son to take away our sins.

Prayer after Communion
Lord,
may this communion so change
 our lives
that we may seek more
 faithfully
the salvation it promises.

Solemn Blessing or Prayer over the People (p.20)

SATURDAY

Your brother was dead and has come to life; he was lost and is found. *The readings today express*

Second Week of Lent: Saturday

the fact that God is a God who forgives without limit or reservation. There can never be any room in the Christian's mind for doubting that God, full of love and compassion, "treads down our faults to the bottom of the sea", once we turn to him and say, "Father, I have sinned".

Entrance Antiphon
The Lord is loving and merciful, to anger slow, and full of love; the Lord is kind to all, and compassionate to all his creatures.

Opening Prayer
God our Father,
by your gifts to us on earth
we already share in your life.
In all we do,
guide us to the light of your kingdom.

Liturgy of the Word
First Reading

A reading from the prophet Micah   7:14-15. 18-20
Tread down our faults to the bottom of the sea.

With shepherd's crook, O Lord,
  lead your people to pasture,
the flock that is your heritage,
living confined in a forest
with meadow land all around.
Let them pasture in Bashan and Gilead
as in the days of old.
As in the days when you came out of Egypt
grant us to see wonders.
What god can compare with you: taking fault away,
pardoning crime,
not cherishing anger for ever
but delighting in showing mercy?
Once more have pity on us,
tread down our faults,
to the bottom of the sea
throw all our sins.
Grant Jacob your faithfulness,
and Abraham your mercy,
as you swore to our fathers
from the days of long ago.

This is the word of the Lord.

Responsorial Psalm   Ps 102:1-4, 9-12. ℟ v.8

℟ The Lord is compassion and love.

1. My soul, gives thanks to the Lord,
  all my being, bless his holy name.
  My soul, give thanks to the Lord
  and never forget all his blessings. ℟

2. It is he who forgives all your guilt,
  who heals every one of your ills,
  who redeems your life from the grave,
  who crowns you with love and compassion. ℟

3. His wrath will come to an end;
  he will not be angry for ever.
  He does not treat us

according to our sins
nor repay us according to
  our faults. ℟

4 For as the heavens are high
    above the earth
  so strong is his love for those
    who fear him.
  As far as the east is from the
    west
  so far does he remove our
    sins. ℟

Gospel Acclamation Lk 15:18
  Glory and praise to you, O
    Christ!
  I will leave this place and go
    to my father and say:
  'Father, I have sinned against
    heaven and against you.'
  Glory and praise to you, O
    Christ!

Gospel

A reading from the holy Gospel according to Luke 15:1-3, 11-32
Your brother here was dead and has come to life.

The tax collectors and the sinners were all seeking the company of Jesus to hear what he had to say, and the Pharisees and the scribes complained. 'This man' they said 'welcomes sinners and eats with them.' So he spoke this parable to them:

'A man had two sons. The younger said to his father, "Father, let me have the share of the estate that would come to me." So the father divided the property between them. A few days later, the younger son got together everything he had and left for a distant country where he squandered his money on a life of debauchery.

'When he had spent it all, that country experienced a severe famine, and now he began to feel the pinch, so he hired himself out to one of the local inhabitants who put him on his farm to feed the pigs. And he would willingly have filled his belly with the husks the pigs were eating but no one offered him anything. Then he came to his senses and said, "How many of my father's paid servants have more food than they want, and here am I dying of hunger! I will leave this place and go to my father and say: Father, I have sinned against heaven and against you; I no longer deserve to be called your son; treat me as one of your paid servants." So he left the place and went back to his father.

'While he was still a long way off, his father saw him and was moved with pity. He ran to the boy, clasped him in his arms and kissed him tenderly. Then his son said, "Father, I have sinned against heaven and against you. I no longer deserve to be called your son." But the father said to his servants. "Quick! Bring out the best robe and put it on him; put a ring on his finger and sandals on his feet. Bring the calf we have been fattening, and kill it, we are going to have a feast, a celebration because this son of mine was dead and has come back to life; he was lost and is found." And they began to celebrate.

'Now the elder son was out in the fields, and on his way back, as he drew near the house, he coud hear music and dancing. Calling one of the servants he asked what it was all about. "Your brother has come" replied the servant "and your father has killed the calf we had fattened because he has got him back safe and sound." He was angry then and refused to go in, and his father came out to plead with him; but he answered his father, "Look, all these years I have slaved for you and never once disobeyed your orders, yet you never offered me so much as a kid for me to celebrate with my friends. But, for this son of yours, when he comes back after swallowing up your property — he and his women — you killed the calf we had been fattening."

'The father said, "My son, you are with me always and all I have is yours. But it was only right we should celebrate and rejoice, because your brother here was dead and has come to life; he was lost and is found." '

This is the Gospel of the Lord.

Prayer over the Gifts
Lord,
may the grace of these sacraments help us to reject all harmful things and lead us to your spiritual gifts.

Preface of Lent I-IV p.8.

Communion Antiphon
My son, you should rejoice, because your brother was dead and has come back to life; he was lost and is found.

Prayer after Communion
Lord,
give us the spirit of love
and lead us to share in your life.

Solemn Blessing or Prayer over the People (p.20)

THIRD WEEK OF LENT

MONDAY

My soul is thirsting for God, the God of my life! *The story of Naaman reminds us that God's call to salvation comes to all without distinction. We were washed clean of all stain in the sacrament of Baptism, and our observance of Lent is a renewal of that cleansing. We must always be open to recognise the will of God even in little things.*

Entrance Antiphon
My soul is longing and pining for the courts of the Lord; my heart and my flesh sing for joy to the living God.

Opening Prayer
God of mercy,
free your Church from sin
and protect it from evil.
Guide us, for we cannot be saved without you.

Liturgy of the Word
First Reading

A reading from the second book of the Kings 5:1-15
There were many lepers in Israel, but none of these was cured, except the Syrian, Naaman.

Naaman, army commander to the king of Aram, was a man who enjoyed his master's respect and favour, since through him the Lord had granted victory to the Aramaeans. But the man was a leper. Now on one of their raids, the Aramaeans had carried off from the land of Israel a little girl who had become a servant of Naaman's wife. She said to her mistress, 'If only my master would approach the prophet of Samaria. He would cure him of his leprosy.' Naaman went and told his master. 'This and this' he reported 'is what the girl from the land of Israel said.' 'Go by all means,' said the king of Aram 'I will send a letter to the king of Israel.' So Naaman left, taking with him ten talents of silver, six thousand shekels of gold and ten festal robes. He presented the letter to the king of Israel. It read: 'With this letter, I am sending my servant Naaman to you for you to cure him of his leprosy.' When the king of Israel read the letter, he tore his garments. 'Am I a god to give death and life,' he said 'that he sends a man to me and asks me to cure him of his leprosy? Listen to this, and take note of it and see how he intends to pick a quarrel with me.'

When Elisha heard that the king of Israel had torn his garments, he sent word to the king, 'Why did you tear your garments? Let him come to me, and he will find there is a prophet in Israel.' So Naaman came with his team and chariot and drew up at the door of Elisha's house. And Elisha sent him a messenger to say, 'Go and bathe seven times in the Jordan, and your flesh will become clean once more.' But Naaman was indignant and went off, saying, 'Here was I thinking he would be sure to come out to me, and stand there, and call on the name of the Lord his God, and wave his hand over the spot and cure the leprous part. Surely Abana and Pharpar, the rivers of Damascus, are better than any water in Israel? Could I not bathe in them and become clean? And he turned round and went off in a rage. But his servants approached him and said, 'My father, if the prophet had asked you to do something difficult, would you not have done it? All the more reason, then, when he says to you, "Bathe and you will become clean." 'So he went down and immersed himself seven times in the Jordan, as Elisha had told him to do. And his flesh became clean once more like the flesh of a little child.

Returning to Elisha with his whole escort, he went in and stood before him. 'Now I know' he said

Third Week of Lent: Monday

'that there is no God in all the earth except in Israel.'

This is the word of the Lord.

Responsorial Psalm   Pss 41:2-3; 42:3-4. ℟ 41:3

℟ **My soul is thirsting for God, the God of my life; when can I enter and see the face of God?**

1 Like the deer that yearns
   for running streams,
   so my soul is yearning
   for you, my God. ℟

2 My soul is thirsting for God,
   the God of my life;
   when can I enter and see
   the face of God? ℟

3 O send forth your light and
      your truth;
   let these be my guide.
   Let them bring me to your
      holy mountain
   to the place where you
      dwell. ℟

4 And I will come to the altar
      of God,
   the God of my joy.
   My redeemer, I will thank
      you on the harp,
   O God, my God. ℟

Gospel Acclamation   2 Cor 6:2
   Praise and honour to you,
      Lord Jesus!
   Now is the favourable time;
   this is the day of salvation.
   Praise and honour to you,
      Lord Jesus!

or   cf. Ps 129:4-7
   Praise and honour to you,
      Lord Jesus!
   My soul is waiting for the
      Lord,
   I count on his word,
   because with the Lord there
      is mercy
   and fullness of redemption.
   Praise and honour to you,
      Lord Jesus!

Gospel

A reading from the holy Gospel according to Luke   4:24-30
Like Elijah and Elisha, Jesus is not sent to the Jews only.

Jesus came to Nazara and spoke to the people in the synagogue: 'I tell you solemnly, no prophet is ever accepted in his own country.

'There were many widows in Israel, I can assure you, in Elijah's day, when heaven remained shut for three years and six months and a great famine raged throughout the land, but Elijah was not sent to any one of these: he was sent to a widow at Zarephath, a Sidonian town. And in the prophet Elisha's time there were many lepers in Israel, but none of these was cured, except the Syrian, Naaman.'

When they heard this everyone in the synagogue was enraged. They sprang to this feet and hustled him out of the town; and they took him up to the brow of the hill their town was built on, intending to throw him down the cliff, but he slipped through the crowd and walked away.

This is the Gospel of the Lord.

Prayer over the Gifts
Father,
bless these gifts
that they may become the
    sacrament of our salvation.

Preface of Lent I-IV p.8.

Communion Antiphon
All you nations, praise the Lord, for
steadfast is his kindly mercy to us.

Prayer after Communion
Lord,
forgive the sins of those
who receive your sacrament,
and bring us together in unity
    and peace.

*Solemn Blessing or Prayer over
    the People (p.20)*

TUESDAY

Forgive your brother from your heart. *One who has suffered real humiliation, poverty and deprivation appreciates the gentle mercy of God when the time of deliverance comes. There should be then only the effort to imitate that gentleness and mercy. We must forgive others from our heart.*

Entrance Antiphon
I call upon you, God, for you will answer me; bend your ear and hear my prayer. Guard me as the pupil of your eye; hide me in the shade of your wings.

Opening Prayer
Lord,
you call us to your service
and continue your saving work
    among us.
May your love never abandon us.

Liturgy of the Word
First Reading

A reading from the prophet Daniel
    3:25.34-43
May the contrite soul, the humbled spirit be acceptable to you.

Azariah stood in the heart of the fire, and he began to pray:

Oh! Do not abandon us for ever,
for the sake of your name;
do not repudiate your covenant,
do not withdraw your favour from us,
for the sake of Abraham, your friend,
of Isaac your servant,
and of Israel your holy one,
to whom you promised
descendants as countless as the stars of heaven,
and as the grains of sand on the seashore.
Lord, now we are the least of all the nations,
now we are despised
throughout the world today
because of our sins.

We have at this time no leader, no prophet, no prince,
no holocaust, no sacrifice, no oblation, no incense,
no place where we can offer you the first-fruits
and win your favour.
But may the contrite soul, the humbled spirit be as acceptable to you
as holocausts of rams and bullocks,
as thousands of fattened lambs:
such let our sacrifice be to you today,
and may it be your will that we follow you wholeheartedly,
since those who put their trust in you will not be disappointed.
And now we put our whole heart into following you,
into fearing you and seeking your face once more.
Do not disappoint us: treat us gently, as you yourself are gentle
and very merciful.
Grant us deliverance worthy of your wonderful deeds,
let your name win glory, Lord.
This is the word of the Lord.

Responsorial Psalm
   Ps 24:4-9. ℟ *v.6*

℟ **Remember your mercy, Lord.**

1 Lord, make me know your ways.
 Lord, teach me your paths.
 Make me walk in your truth, and teach me:
 for you are God my saviour. ℟

2 Remember your mercy, Lord, and the love you have shown from of old.
 Do not remember the sins of my youth
 because of your goodness, O Lord. ℟

3 The Lord is good and upright.
 He shows the path to those who stray.
 He guides the humble in the right path;
 he teaches his way to the poor. ℟

Gospel Acclamation   *cf. Lk 8:15*
 Glory and praise to you, O Christ!
 Blessed are those who, with a noble and generous heart,
 take the word of God to themselves
 and yield a harvest through their perseverance.
 Glory and praise to you, O Christ!

or   *Joel 2:12-13*
 Glory and praise to you, O Christ!
 Now, now — it is the Lord who speaks —
 come back to me with all your heart,

for I am all tenderness and
  compassion.
Glory and praise to you, O
  Christ!

Gospel

A reading from the holy Gospel according to Matthew   18:21-35
Your Father will not forgive you unless you each forgive your brother from your heart.

Peter went up to Jesus and said, 'Lord, how often must I forgive my brother if he wrongs me? As often as seven times?' Jesus answered, 'Not seven, I tell you, but seventy-seven times.

  'And so the kingdom of heaven may be compared to a king who decided to settle his accounts with his servants. When the reckoning began, they brought him a man who owed ten thousand talents; but he had no means of paying, so his master gave orders that he should be sold, together with his wife and children and all his possessions, to meet the debt. At this, the servant threw himself down at his master's feet. "Give me time" he said "and I will pay the whole sum." And the servant's master felt so sorry for him that he let him go and cancelled the debt. Now as this servant went out, he happened to meet a fellow servant who owed him one hundred denarii; and he seized him by the throat and began to throttle him. "Pay what you owe me" he said. His fellow servant fell at his feet and implored him, saying, "Give me time and I will pay you." But the other would not agree; on the contrary, he had him thrown into prison till he should pay the debt. His fellow servants were deeply distressed when they saw what had happened, and they went to their master and reported the whole affair to him. Then the master sent for him. "You wicked servant," he said. "I cancelled all that debt of yours when you appealed to me. Were you not bound, then, to have pity on your fellow servant just as I had pity on you?" And in his anger the master handed him over to the torturers till he should pay all his debt. And that is how my heavenly Father will deal with you unless you each forgive your brother from your heart.'

  This is the Gospel of the Lord.

Prayer over the Gifts
Lord,
may the saving sacrifice we offer bring us your forgiveness,
so that freed from sin, we may
  always please you.

Preface of Lent I-IV p.8.

Communion Antiphon
Lord, who may stay in your dwelling place? Who shall live on your holy mountain? He who walks without blame and does what is right.

Third Week of Lent: Wednesday

Prayer after Communion
Lord,
may our sharing in this holy mystery
bring us your protection, forgiveness and life.

Solemn Blessing or Prayer over the People (p.20)

WEDNESDAY

Take notice of the laws and observe them. *There is a place for laws and commandments in the life of the Christian. Moses called on the people to be proud of the fact that they had a God who gave them such a collection of laws. Observing these laws was a way of praising God. Following Christ means loving his law. Observing the law is the way to heaven.*

Entrance Antiphon
Lord, direct my steps as you have promised, and let no evil hold me in its power.

Opening Prayer
Lord,
during this lenten season
nourish us with your word of life
and make us one in love and prayer.

Liturgy of the Word
First Reading

A reading from the book of Deuteronomy 4:1. 5-9
Take notice of the laws and observe them.

Moses said to the people: 'And now, Israel, take notice of the laws and customs that I teach you today, and observe them, that you may have life and may enter and take possession of the land that the Lord the God of your fathers is giving you. See, as the Lord my God has commanded me, I teach you the laws and customs that you are to observe in the land you are to enter and make your own. Keep them, observe them, and they will demonstrate to the peoples your wisdom and understanding. When they come to know of all these laws they will exclaim, "No other people is as wise and prudent as this great nation." And indeed, what great nation is there that has its gods so near as the Lord our God is to us whenever we call to him? And what great nation is there that has laws and customs to match this whole Law that I put before you today?

'But take care what you do and be on your guard. Do not forget the things your eyes have seen, nor let them slip from your heart all the days of your life; rather, tell them to your children and to your children's children.'

This is the word of the Lord.

Responsorial Psalm
Ps 147:12-13. 15-16. 19-20.
℟ v.12
℟ O praise the Lord, Jerusalem!

1 O praise the Lord, Jerusalem!
   Zion, praise your God!

He has strengthened the bars of your gates,
he has blessed the children within you. ℟

2   He sends out his word to the earth
and swiftly runs his command.
He showers down snow white as wool,
he scatters hoar-frost like ashes. ℟

3   He makes his word known to Jacob,
to Israel his laws and decrees.
He has not dealt thus with other nations;
he has not taught them his decrees. ℟

Gospel Acclamation   Jn 8:12
Glory to you, O Christ, you are the Word of God!
I am the light of the world, says the Lord,
anyone who follows me will have the light of life.
Glory to you, O Christ, you are the Word of God!

or   cf. Jn 6:63, 68

Glory to you, O Christ, you are the Word of God!
Your words are spirit, Lord, and they are life;
you have the message of eternal life.
Glory to you, O Christ, you are the Word of God!

Gospel

A reading from the holy Gospel according to Matthew   5:17-19
The man who keeps these commandments and teaches them will be considered great in the kingdom of heaven.

Jesus said to his disciples: 'Do not imagine that I have come to abolish the Law or the Prophets. I have come not to abolish but to complete them. I tell you solemnly, till heaven and earth disappear, not one dot, not one little stroke, shall disappear from the Law until its purpose is achieved. Therefore, the man who infringes even one of the least of these commandments and teaches others to do the same will be considered the least in the kingdom of heaven; but the man who keeps them and teaches them will be considered great in the kingdom of heaven.'

This is the Gospel of the Lord.

Prayer over the Gifts
Lord,
receive our prayers and offerings.
In time of danger,
protect all who celebrate this sacrament.

Preface of Lent I-IV. p.8

Communion Antiphon
Lord, you will show me the path of life and fill me with joy in your presence.

Prayer after Communion
Lord,
may this eucharist forgive our sins,
make us holy,
and prepare us for the eternal life you promise.

Solemn Blessing or Prayer over the People (p.20)

THURSDAY

He who is not with me is against me. *Despite all God's revelation people still seek signs and wonders, and persistently find excuses for not believing. Jesus calls for a total response to his call. That response must be made now, we cannot delay and allow our hearts to be hardened. Lent is the time of salvation.*

Entrance Antiphon
I am the Saviour of all people, says the Lord. Whatever their troubles, I will answer their cry; and I will always be their Lord.

Opening Prayer
Father,
help us to be ready to celebrate the great paschal mystery.
Make our love grow each day
as we approach the feast of our salvation.

Liturgy of the Word
First Reading

A reading from the prophet Jeremiah 7:23-28

Here is the nation that will not listen to the voice of the Lord its God.

These were my orders: Listen to my voice, then I will be your God and you shall be my people. Follow right to the end the way that I mark out for you, and you will prosper. But they did not listen, they did not pay attention; they followed the dictates of their own evil hearts, refused to face me, and turned their backs on me from the day your ancestors came out of the land of Egypt until today; day after day I have persistently sent you all my servants the prophets. But they have not listened to me, have not paid attention; they have grown stubborn and behaved worse than their ancestors. You may say all these words to them: they will not listen to you; you may call them: they will not answer. So tell them this, 'Here is the nation that will not listen to the voice of the Lord its God nor take correction. Sincerity is no more, it has vanished from their mouths.'

This is the word of the Lord.

Responsorial Psalm
Ps 94:1-2, 6-9. ℟ v.8
℟ **O that today you would listen to his voice!
'Harden not your hearts.'**

1 Come, ring out our joy to the Lord;
   hail the rock who saves us.

Let us come before him,
  giving thanks,
with songs let us hail the
  Lord. ℟

2 Come in; let us bow and
    bend low;
  let us kneel before the God
    who made us
  for he is our God and we
  the people who belong to his
    pasture,
  the flock that is led by his
    hand. ℟

3 O that today you would
    listen to his voice!
  'Harden not your hearts as at
    Meribah,
  as on that day at Massah in
    the desert
  when your fathers put me to
    the test;
  when they tried me, though
    they saw my work.' ℟

Gospel Acclamation   *Ez 18:31*

Praise to you, O Christ, king
  of eternal glory!
Shake off all your sins — it is
  the Lord who speaks —
and make yourselves a new
  heart and a new spirit.
Praise to you, O Christ, king
  of eternal glory!

or   *Joel 2:12-13*

Praise to you, O Christ, king
  of eternal glory!
Now, now — it is the Lord
  who speaks —
come back to me with all
  your heart,
for I am all tenderness and
  compassion.
Praise to you, O Christ, king
  of eternal glory!

Gospel

A reading from the holy Gospel
according to Luke   *11:14-23*
*He who is not with me is against
me.*

Jesus was casting out a devil and
it was dumb; but when the devil
had gone out the dumb man
spoke, and the people were
amazed. But some of them said, 'It
is through Beelzebub, the prince
of devils, that he casts out devils.'
Others asked him, as a test, for a
sign from heaven; but, knowing
what they were thinking, he said
to them, 'Every kingdom divided
against itself is heading for ruin,
and a household divided against
itself collapses. So too with Satan:
if he is divided against himself, how
can his kingdom stand? — since
you assert that it is through
Beelzebub that I cast out devils.
Now if it is through Beelzebub that
I cast out devils through whom do
your own experts cast them out?
Let them be your judges, then. But
if it is through the finger of God
that I cast out devils, then know
that the kingdom of God has
overtaken you. So long as a strong
man fully armed guards his own
palace, his goods are undisturbed;
but when someone stronger than
he is attacks and defeats him, the

stronger man takes away all the weapons he relied on and shares out his spoil.

'He who is not with me is against me; and he who does not gather with me scatters.'

This is the Gospel of the Lord.

Prayer over the Gifts
Lord,
take away our sinfulness and be pleased with our offerings.
Help us to pursue the true gifts you promise
and not become lost in false joys.

Preface of Lent I-IV p.8.

Communion Antiphon
You have laid down your precepts to be faithfully kept. May my footsteps be firm in keeping your commands.

Prayer after Communion
Lord,
may your sacrament of life
bring us the gift of salvation
and make our lives pleasing to you.

Solemn Blessing or Prayer over the People (p.20)

FRIDAY

Let there be no foreign god among you, no worship of an alien god.
Jesus has reduced all the books of laws and commandments to just two: love of God and love of neighbour. So we are to worship that one God, and no other idol is to have a place in our lives. Even if we have failed in this his word still stands before us: "Come back to the Lord your God".

Entrance Antiphon
Lord, there is no god to compare with you; you are great and do wonderful things, you are the only God.

Opening Prayer
Merciful Father,
fill our hearts with your love
and keep us faithful to the gospel of Christ.
Give us the grace to rise above our human weakness.

Liturgy of the Word
First Reading

A reading from the prophet Hosea   14:2-10
We will not say any more, 'Our God' to what our own hands have made.

The Lord says this:
  Israel, come back to the Lord your God;
  your iniquity was the cause of your downfall.
  Provide yourself with words and come back to the Lord.
  Say to him, 'Take all iniquity away
  so that we may have happiness again
  and offer you our words of praise.

Assyria cannot save us,
we will not ride horses any
 more,
or say, "Our God!" to what
 our own hands have made,
for you are the one in whom
 orphans find compassion.'
— I will heal their disloyalty,
I will love them with all my
 heart,
for my anger has turned from
 them.
I will fall like dew on Israel.
He shall bloom like the lily,
and thrust out roots like the
 poplar,
his shoots will spread far;
he will have the beauty of
 the olive
and the fragrance of
 Lebanon.
They will come back to live
 in my shade;
they will grow corn that
 flourishes,
they will cultivate vines
as renowned as the wine of
 Helbon.
What has Ephraim to do with
 idols any more
when it is I who hear his
 prayer and care for him?
I am like a cypress ever
 green,
all your fruitfulness comes
 from me.
Let the wise man understand
 these words.
Let the intelligent man grasp
 their meaning.
For the ways of the Lord are
 straight,
and virtuous men walk in
 them,
but sinners stumble.

This is the word of the Lord.

Responsorial Psalm Ps 80:6, 8-11, 14, 17. ℟ v.v.9, 11

℟ **I am the Lord your God;
listen to my warning.**

1 A voice I did not know said
  to me:
  'I freed your shoulder from
   the burden;
  your hands were freed from
   the load.
  You called in distress and I
   saved you. ℟

2 'I answered, concealed in the
   storm cloud,
  at the waters of Meribah I
   tested you.
  Listen, my people, to my
   warning,
  O Israel, if only you would
   heed! ℟

3 'Let there be no foreign god
   among you,
  no worship of an alien god.
  I am the Lord your God,
  who brought you from the
   land of Egypt. ℟

4 'O that my people would
   heed me,
  that Israel would walk in my
   ways!
  But Israel I would feed with
   finest wheat
  and fill them with honey
   from the rock.' ℟

Third Week of Lent: Friday

Gospel Acclamation
> Praise and honour to you,
>   Lord Jesus!
> The seed is the word of God,
>   Christ the sower;
> whoever finds this seed will
>   remain for ever.
> Praise and honour to you,
>   Lord Jesus!

or   Mt 4:17

> Praise and honour to you,
>   Lord Jesus!
> Repent, says the Lord,
> for the kingdom of heaven is
>   close at hand.
> Praise and honour to you,
>   Lord Jesus!

Gospel

A reading from the holy Gospel according to Mark   12:28-34
The Lord our God is the one Lord, and you must love him.

One of the scribes came up to Jesus and put a question to him, 'Which is the first of all the commandments?' Jesus replied, 'This is the first: Listen, Israel, the Lord our God is the one Lord, and you must love the Lord your God with all your heart, with all your soul, with all your mind, and with all your strength. The second is this: You must love your neighbour as yourself. There is no commandment greater than these.' The scribe said to him, 'Well spoken, Master; what you have said is true: that he is one and there is no other. To love him with all your heart, with all your understanding and strength, and to love your neighbour as yourself, this is far more important than any holocaust or sacrifice.' Jesus, seeing how wisely he had spoken, said, 'You are not far from the kingdom of God.' And after that no one dared to question him any more.

This is the Gospel of the Lord.

Prayer over the Gifts
Lord,
bless the gifts we have prepared.
Make them acceptable to you and a lasting source of salvation.

Preface of Lent I-IV. p.8.

Communion Antiphon
To love God with all your heart, and your neighbour as yourself, is a greater thing than all the temple sacrifices.

Prayer after Communion
Lord,
fill us with the power of your love.
As we share in this eucharist, may we come to know fully the redemption we have received.

Solemn Blessing or Prayer over the People (p.20)

SATURDAY
God, be merciful to me, a sinner!

Good works are not bribes to God for our salvation, rather they are the result of lives lived for God. God wants the love of contrite humble hearts, not mere external observances. He wants a faithful love, not one that fades like the dew in the morning sun.

Entrance Antiphon
Bless the Lord, my soul, and remember all his kindnesses, for he pardons all my faults.

Opening Prayer
Lord,
make this lenten observance
of the suffering, death and resurrection of Christ
bring us to the full joy of Easter.

Liturgy of the Word
First Reading

A reading from the prophet Hosea   5:15-6:6
What I want is love, not sacrifice.

The Lord says this:
    They will search for me in their misery:
    'Come, let us return to the Lord.
    He has torn us to pieces, but he will heal us;
    he has struck us down, but he will bandage our wounds;
    after a day or two he will bring us back to life,
    on the third day he will raise us
    and we shall live in his presence.
    Let us set ourselves to know the Lord;
    that he will come is as certain as the dawn,
    he will come to us as showers come,
    like spring rains watering the earth.

    What am I to do with you, Ephraim?
    What am I to do with you, Judah?
    This love of yours is like a morning cloud,
    like the dew that quickly disappears.
    This is why I have torn them to pieces by the prophets,
    why I slaughtered them with the words from my mouth,
    his judgement will rise like the light,
    since what I want is love, not sacrifice;
    knowledge of God, not holocausts.

This is the word of the Lord.

Responsorial Psalm   Ps 50:3-4. 18-21. ℟ cf. Hos 6:6

℟ What I want is love, not sacrifice.

1 Have mercy on me, God, in your kindness.
    In your compassion blot out my offence.

Third Week of Lent: Saturday

O wash me more and more from my guilt
and cleanse me from my sin. ℟

2. For in sacrifice you take no delight,
burnt offering from me you would refuse,
my sacrifice, a contrite spirit.
A humbled, contrite heart you will not spurn. ℟

3. In your goodness, show favour to Zion:
rebuild the walls of Jerusalem.
Then you will be pleased with lawful sacrifice,
burnt offerings wholly consumed. ℟

Gospel Acclamation cf. Ps 94:8
Glory and praise to you, O Christ!
Harden not your hearts today,
but listen to the voice of the Lord.
Glory and praise to you, O Christ!

Gospel

A reading from the holy Gospel according to Luke 18:9-14
The tax collector went home again at rights with God; the Pharisee did not.

Jesus spoke the following parable to some people who prided themselves on being virtuous and despised everyone else. 'Two men went up to the Temple to pray, one a Pharisee, the other a tax collector. The Pharisee stood there and said this prayer to himself, "I thank you, God, that I am not grasping, unjust, adulterous like the rest of mankind, and particularly that I am not like this tax collector here. I fast twice a week; I pay tithes on all I get." The tax collector stood some distance away, not daring even to raise his eyes to heaven; but he beat his breast and said, "God, be merciful to me, a sinner." This man, I tell you, went home again at rights with God; the other did not. For everyone who exalts himself will be humbled, but the man who humbles himself will be exalted.'

This is the Gospel of the Lord.

Prayer over the Gifts
Lord,
by your grace you enable us to come to these mysteries with renewed lives.
May this eucharist give you worthy praise.

Preface of Lent I-IV. p.8.

Prayer after Communion
God of mercy,
may the holy gifts we receive help us to worship you in truth,
and to receive your sacraments with faith.

Solemn Blessing or Prayer over the People (p.20)

FOURTH WEEK OF LENT
MONDAY

I will praise you, Lord, you have rescued me. Remorse and anxiety are signs of weak faith in God's forgiveness. Genuine repentance brings joy. The rescued break out into praise of God. The signs that Jesus worked were to help us to come to strong faith. Joy and gladness should characterise Christians who have been given the pledge of eternal life in Baptism.

Entrance Antiphon
Lord, I put my trust in you; I shall be glad and rejoice in your mercy, because you have seen my affliction.

Opening Prayer
Father, creator,
you give the world new life by your sacraments.
May we, your Church, grow in your life
and continue to receive your help on earth.

Liturgy of the Word
First Reading

A reading from the prophet Isaiah
65:17-21
No more will the sound of weeping or the sound of cries be heard.

Thus says the Lord: Now I create new heavens and a new earth, and the past will not be remembered, and will come no more to men's minds. Be glad and rejoice for ever and ever for what I am creating, because I now create Jerusalem 'Joy' and her people 'Gladness', I shall rejoice over Jerusalem and exult in my people. No more will the sound of weeping or the sound of cries be heard in her; in her, no more will be found the infant living a few days only, or the old man not living to the end of his days. To die at the age of a hundred will be dying young; not to live to be a hundred will be the sign of a curse. They will build houses and inhabit them, plant vineyards and eat their fruit.

This is the word of the Lord.

Responsorial Psalm Ps 29:2. 4-6. 11-13. ℟ v.2

℟ I will praise you, Lord, you have rescued me.

1 I will praise you, Lord, you have rescued me
   and have not let my enemies rejoice over me
   O Lord, you have raised my soul from the dead,
   restored me to life from those who sink into the grave. ℟

2 Sing psalms to the Lord, you who love him,
   give thanks to his holy name.
   His anger lasts but a moment; his favour through life.
   At night there are tears, but joy comes with dawn. ℟

Fourth Week of Lent: Monday

3 The Lord listened and had pity.
The Lord came to my help.
For me you have changed my mourning into dancing;
O Lord my God, I will thank you for ever. ℟

Gospel Acclamation
cf. Ps 129:5. 7

Praise and honour to you, Lord Jesus!
My soul is waiting for the Lord.
I count on his word,
because with the Lord there is mercy
and fullness of redemption.
Praise and honour to you, Lord Jesus!

or cf. Amos 5:14

Praise and honour to you, Lord Jesus!
Seek good and not evil so that you may live,
and that the Lord God of hosts may really be with you.
Praise and honour to you, Lord Jesus!

Gospel

A reading from the holy Gospel according to John 4:43-45
Go home, your son will live.

Jesus left Samaria for Galilee. He himself had declared that there is no respect for a prophet in his own country, but on his arrival the Galileans received him well, having seen all that he had done at Jerusalem during the festival which they too had attended.

He went again to Cana in Galilee, where he had changed the water into wine. Now there was a court official there whose son was ill at Capernaum and, hearing that Jesus had arrived in Galilee from Judaea, he went and asked him to come and cure his son as he was at the point of death. Jesus said, 'So you will not believe unless you see signs and portents!' 'Sir,' answered the official 'come down before my child dies.' 'Go home,' said Jesus 'your son will live.' The man believed what Jesus had said and started on his way; and while he was still on the journey back his servants met him with the news that his boy was alive. He asked them when the boy had begun to recover. 'The fever left him yesterday' they said 'at the seventh hour.' The father realised that this was exactly the time when Jesus had said, 'Your son will live'; and he and all his household believed.

This was the second sign given by Jesus, on his return from Judaea to Galilee.

This is the Gospel of the Lord.

Prayer over the Gifts
Lord,
through the gifts we present
may we receive the grace
to cast off the old ways of life
and to redirect our course
toward the life of heaven.

Preface of Lent I-IV. p.8.

Communion Antiphon
I shall put my spirit within you, says the Lord; you will obey my laws and keep my decrees.

Prayer after Communion
Lord,
may your gifts bring us life and holiness
and lead us to the happiness of eternal life.

Solemn Blessing or Prayer over the People (p.20)

TUESDAY

Be sure not to sin any more, or something worse may happen to you. Jesus takes the initiative in healing the man at the poolside. He commands him to get up and walk. He does this even against Sabbath regulations. And he tells the man that to sin is a worse tragedy than being ill. The waters of Baptism that give joy to the new Jerusalem are given to us as free gift. Through them we accept the commands of Jesus for true living. To sin and lose all would be the worst tragedy.

Entrance Antiphon
Come to the waters, all who thirst; though you have no money, come and drink with joy.

Opening Prayer
Father,
may our lenten observance
prepare us to embrace the paschal mystery
and to proclaim your salvation with joyful praise.

Liturgy of the Word
First Reading

A reading from the prophet Ezekiel
47:1-9. 12
I saw a stream of water coming from the Temple, bringing life to all wherever it flowed.

The angel brought me to the entrance of the Temple, where a stream came out from under the Temple threshold and flowed eastwards, since the Temple faced east. The water flowed from under the right side of the Temple, south of the altar. He took me out by the north gate and led me right round outside as far as the outer east gate where the water flowed out on the right-hand side. The man went to the east holding his measuring line and measured off a thousand cubits; he then made me wade across the stream; the water reached my ankles. He measured off another thousand and made me wade across the stream again; the water reached my knees. He measured off another thousand and made me wade across again; the water reached my waist. He measured off another thousand; it was now a river which I could not cross; the stream had swollen and was now deep water, a river impossible to cross. He then said, 'Do you see, son of man?' He took me further, then brought me back to the bank of the river. When I got back, there were many trees on each bank of the river. He said, 'This water flows east down to the Arabah and to the sea; and flowing into the sea it makes its waters wholesome. Wherever the river flows, all living creatures teeming in it will live. Fish will be very plentiful, for wherever the water goes it brings health, and life teems wherever the river flows. Along the river, on either bank, will grow every kind of fruit tree with leaves that never wither and fruit that never fails; they will bear new fruit every month, because this water comes from the sanctuary. And their fruit will be good to eat and the leaves medicinal.

This is the word of the Lord.

Responsorial Psalm
    Ps 45:2-3, 5-6, 8-9. ℟ *v.8*
℟ **The Lord of hosts is with us: the God of Jacob is our stronghold.**

1 God is for us a refuge and strength,
    a helper close at hand, in time of distress:
  so we shall not fear though the earth should rock,
    though the mountains fall into the depth of the sea. ℟

2 The waters of a riven give joy to God's city,
    the holy place where the Most High dwells.
  God is within, it cannot be shaken;
    God will help it at the dawning of the day. ℟

3 The Lord of hosts is with us:
    the God of Jacob is our stronghold.
  Come, consider the works of the Lord
    the redoubtable deeds he has done on the earth. ℟

Gospel Acclamation Ps 50:12. 14
Praise and honour to you, Lord Jesus!
A pure heart create for me, O God,
and give me again the joy of your help.
Praise and honour to you, Lord Jesus!

Gospel

A reading from the holy Gospel according to John   5:1-3. 5-16
The man was cured at once.

There was a Jewish festival, and Jesus went up to Jerusalem. Now at the Sheep Pool in Jerusalem there is a building, called Bethzatha in Hebrew, consisting of five porticos; and under these were crowds of sick people — blind, lame, paralysed. One man there had an illness which had lasted thirty-eight years, and when Jesus saw him lying there and knew he had been in this condition for a long time, he said, 'Do you want to be well again?' 'Sir,' replied the sick man 'I have no one to put me into the pool when the water is disturbed; and while I am still on the way, someone else gets there before me.' Jesus said 'Get up, pick up your sleeping-mat and walk.' The man was cured at once, and he picked up his mat and walked away.

Now that day happened to be the sabbath, so the Jews said to the man who had been cured, 'It is the sabbath,; you are not allowed to carry your sleeping-mat.' He replied, 'But the man who cured me told me, "Pick up your mat and walk." ' They asked, 'Who is the man who said to you, "Pick up your mat and walk"?' The man had no idea who it was since Jesus had disappeared into the crowd that filled the place. After a while Jesus met him in the Temple and said, 'Now you are well again, be sure not to sin any more, or something worse may happen to you.' The man went back and told the Jews that it was Jesus who had cured him. It was because he did things like this on the sabbath that the Jews began to persecute Jesus.

This the Gospel of the Lord.

Prayer over the Gifts
Lord,
may your gifts of bread and wine
which nourish us here on earth
become the food of our eternal life.

Preface of Lent I-IV. p.8.

Communion Antiphon
The Lord is my shepherd; there is nothing I shall want. In green pastures he gives me rest, he leads me beside the waters of peace.

Prayer after Communion
Lord,
may your holy sacraments
   cleanse and renew us;
may they bring us your help
and lead us to salvation.

Solemn Blessing or Prayer over the People (p.20)

WEDNESDAY

Yet even if these forget, I will never forget you. *Jesus Christ is the source of life for us. Salvation is no longer in the future, it is here already for us in the Christian life. The Lord consoles his people and gives them joy. He will never forget us, he is faithful in all his words. We must listen to his words and believe in him.*

Entrance Antiphon
I pray to you, O God, for the time of your favour. Lord, in your great love, answer me.

Opening Prayer
Lord,
you reward virtue
and forgive the repentant sinner.
Grant us your forgiveness
as we come before you
   confessing our guilt.

Fourth Week of Lent: Wednesday

Liturgy of the Word
First Reading

A reading from the prophet Isaiah   49:8-15

I have appointed you as covenant of the people to restore the land.

Thus says the Lord:
  At the favourable time I will answer you,
  on the day of salvation I will help you.
  (I have formed you and have appointed you
  as covenant of the people.)
  I will restore the land
  and assign you the estates that lie waste.
  I will say to the prisoners, 'Come out',
  to those who are in darkness, 'Show yourselves'.

  On every roadway they will graze,
  and each bare height shall be their pasture.
  They will never hunger or thirst,
  scorching wind and sun shall never plague them;
  for he who pities them will lead them
  and guide them to springs of water.
  I will make a highway of all the mountains,
  and the high roads shall be banked up.
  Some are on their way from afar,
  others from the north and the west,
  others from the land of Sinim.
  Shourt for joy, you heavens;
  exult, you earth!
  You mountains, break into happy cries!
  For the Lord consoles his people
  and takes pity on those who are afflicted.

  For Zion was saying, 'The Lord has abandoned me,
  the Lord has forgotten me.'
  Does a woman forget her baby at the breast,
  or fail to cherish the son of her womb?
  Yet even if these forget,
  I will never forget you.

This is the word of the Lord.

Responsorial Psalm   Ps 144:8-9. 13-14. 17-18. ℟ v.8

℟ The Lord is kind and full of compassion.

1 The Lord is kind and full of compassion,
  slow to anger, abounding in love.
  How good is the Lord to all,
  compassionate to all his creatures. ℟

2 The Lord is faithful in all his words
  and loving in all his deeds.
  The Lord supports all who fall
  and raises all who are bowed down. ℟

3 The Lord is just in all his ways
and loving in all his deeds.
He is close to all who call him,
who call on him from their hearts. ℟

Gospel Acclamation   Jn 3:16

Glory and praise to you, O Christ!
God loved the world so much that he gave his only Son;
everyone who believes in him has eternal life.
Glory and praise to you, O Christ!

or   Jn 11:25-26

Glory and praise to you, O Christ!
I am the resurrection and the life, says the Lord;
whoever believes in me will never die.
Glory and praise to you, O Christ!

Gospel

A reading from the holy Gospel according to John   5:17-30
As the Father raises the dead and gives them life, so the Son gives life to those he chooses.

Jesus said to the Jews: 'My Father goes on working, and so do I.' But that only made the Jews even more intent on killing him, because, not content with breaking the sabbath, he spoke of God as his own Father, and so made himself God's equal. To this accusation Jesus replied:

'I tell you most solemnly,
the Son can do nothing by himself;
he can do only what he sees the Father doing;
and whatever the Father does the Son does too.
For the Father loves the Son
and shows him everything he does himself,
and he will show him even greater things than these,
works that will astonish you.
Thus, as the Father raises the dead and gives them life,
so the Son gives life to anyone he chooses;
for the Father judges no one;
he has entrusted all judgement to the Son,
so that all may honour the Son
as they honour the Father.
Whoever refuses honour to the Son
refuses honour to the Father who sent him.
I tell you most solemnly,
whoever listens to my words,
and believes in the one who sent me,
has eternal life;
without being brought to judgement
he has passed from death to life.
I tell you most solemnly,
the hour will come — in fact it is here already —

when the dead will hear the voice of the Son of God,
and all who hear it will live.
For the Father, who is the source of life,
has made the Son the source of life;
and, because he is the Son of Man,
has appointed him supreme judge.
Do not be surprised at this,
for the hour is coming
when the dead will leave their graves
at the sound of his voice:
those who did good
will rise again to life;
and those who did evil, to condemnation.
I can do nothing by myself;
I can only judge as I am told to judge,
and my judging is just,
because my aim is to do not my own will,
but the will of him who sent me.'

Prayer over the Gifts
Lord God,
may the power of this sacrifice wash away our sins,
renew our lives and bring us to salvation.

Preface of Lent I-IV. p.8.

Communion Antiphon
God sent his Son into the world, not to condemn it, but so that the world might be saved through him.

Prayer after Communion
Lord,
may we never misuse your healing gifts,
but always find in them a source of life and salvation.

Solemn Blessing or Prayer over the People (p.20)

THURSDAY

O Lord, remember me out of the love you have for your people.
Again and again human beings raise up idols of their own making and give them the worship due to God. Moses on the occasion of the apostasy of his people pleaded to God for their forgiveness, and God heard his plea. We have to put our trust in Jesus who makes intercession for us before the Father.

Entrance Antiphon
Let hearts rejoice who search for the Lord. Seek the Lord and his strength, seek always the face of the Lord.

Opening Prayer
Merciful Father,
may the penance of our lenten observance
make us your obedient people.
May the love within us be seen in what we do
and lead us to the joy of Easter.

Liturgy of the Word
First Reading

A reading from the book of Exodus
32:7-14
Do not bring this disaster on your people.

The Lord spoke to Moses. 'Go down now, because your people whom you brought out of Egypt have apostasised. They have been quick to leave the way I marked out for them; they have made themselves a calf of molten metal and have worshipped it and offered it sacrifice. "Here is your God, Israel," they have cried "who brought you up from the land of Egypt!" I can see how headstrong these people are! Leave me now, my wrath shall blaze out against them and devour them; of you, however, I will make a great nation.'

But Moses pleaded with the Lord his God. 'Lord,' he said 'why should your wrath blaze out against this people of yours whom you brought out of the land of Egypt with arm outstretched and mighty hand? Why let the Egyptians say, "Ah, it was in treachery that he brought them out, to do them to death in the mountains and wipe them off the face of the earth"? Leave your burning wrath; relent and do not bring this disaster on your people. Remember Abraham, Isaac and Jacob, your servants to whom by your own self you swore and made this promise: I will make your offspring as many as the stars of heaven, and all this land which I promised I will give to your descendants, and it shall be their heritage for ever.' So the Lord relented and did not bring on his people the disaster he had threatened.

This is the word of the Lord.

Responsorial Psalm Ps 105:19-23.
℟ v.4

℟ **O Lord, remember me out of the love you have for your people.**

1 They fashioned a calf at Horeb
  and worshipped an image of metal,
  exchanging the God who was their glory
  for the image of a bull that eats grass. ℟

2 They forgot the God who was their saviour,
  who had done such great things in Egypt,
  such portents in the land of Ham,
  such marvels at the Red Sea. ℟

3 For this he said he would destroy them,
  but Moses, the man he had chosen,
  stood in the breach before him,
  to turn back his anger from destruction. ℟

Fourth Week of Lent: Thursday

Gospel Acclamation

cf. Jn 6:63, 68

Glory to you, O Christ, you are the Word of God!
Your words are spirit, Lord, and they are life;
you have the message of eternal life.
Glory to you, O Christ, you are the Word of God!

or   Jn 3:16

Glory to you, O Christ, you are the Word of God!
God loved the world so much that he gave his only Son,
everyone who believes in him has eternal life.
Glory to you, O Christ, you are the Word of God!

Gospel

A reading from the holy Gospel according to John   5:31-47
You place your hope in Moses, and Moses will be your accuser.

Jesus said to the Jews.

'Were I to testify on my own behalf,
my testimony would not be valid,
but there is another witness who can speak on my behalf,
and I know that his testimony is valid.
You sent messengers to John, and he gave his testimony to the truth:
not that I depend on human testimony;
no, it is for your salvation that I speak of this.

John was a lamp alight and shining
and for a time you were content to enjoy the light that he gave.
But my testimony is greater than John's:
the works my Father has given me to carry out,
these same works of mine testify that the Father has sent me.
Besides, the Father who sent me
bears witness to me himself.
You have never heard his voice,
you have never seen his shape,
and his word finds no home in you
because you do not believe in the one he has sent.

'You study the scriptures,
believing that in them you have eternal life;
now these same scriptures testify to me
and yet you refuse to come to me for life!
As for human approval, this means nothing to me.
Besides, I know you too well:
you have no love of God in you.
I have come in the name of my Father
and you refuse to accept me;

if someone else comes in his own name
you will accept him.

'How can you believe,
since you look to one another for approval
and are not concerned
with the approval that comes from the one God?
Do not imagine that I am going to accuse you before the Father:
you place your hopes on Moses,
and Moses will be your accuser.
If you really believed him
you would believe me too,
since it was I that he was writing about;
but if you refuse to believe what he wrote,
how can you believe what I say?'

This is the Gospel of the Lord.

Prayer over the Gifts
All-powerful God,
look upon our weaknesses.
May the sacrifice we offer
bring us purity and strength.

Preface of Lent I-IV. p.8.

Communion Antiphon
I will put my law within them, I will write it on their hearts; then I shall be their God, and they will be my people.

Prayer after Communion
Lord,
may the sacraments we receive
cleanse us of sin and free us from guilt,
for our sins bring us sorrow
but your promise of salvation brings us joy.

Solemn Blessing or Prayer over the People (p.20)

FRIDAY

The Lord is close to the brokenhearted. *Jesus meets opposition in Jerusalem; he is disliked because he is a Galilean, because his origins are so ordinary. The book of Wisdom points out that such a just man always stands as a reproof to others. He points out their defects simply by his own goodness. He is a threat that has to be removed, even by a violent death.*

Entrance Antiphon
Save me, O God, by your power, and grant me justice! God, hear my prayer; listen to my plea.

Opening Prayer
Father, our source of life,
you know our weakness.
May we reach out with joy to grasp your hand
and walk more readily in your ways.

Liturgy of the Word
First Reading

A reading from the book of Wisdom   2:1.12-22

Let us condemn him to a shameful death.

The godless say to themselves, with their misguided reasoning:

> 'Let us lie in wait for the virtuous man, since he annoys us
> and opposes our way of life,
> reproaches us for our breaches of the law
> and accuses us of playing false to our upbringing.
> He claims to have a knowledge of God,
> and calls himself a son of the Lord.
> Before us he stands, a reproof to our way of thinking,
> the very sight of him weighs our spirits down,
> his way of life is not like other men's,
> the paths he treads are unfamiliar.
> In his opinion we are counterfeit;
> he holds aloof from our doings as though from filth;
> he proclaims the final end of the virtuous as happy
> and boasts of having God for his father.
> Let us see if what he says is true,
> let us observe what kind of end he himself will have.
> If the virtuous man is God's son, God will take his part
> and rescue him from the clutches of his enemies.
> Let us test him with cruelty and with torture,
> and thus explore this gentleness of his
> and put his endurance to the proof.
> Let us condemn him to a shameful death
> since he will be looked after — we have his word for it.'

This is the way they reason, but they are misled,
their malice makes them blind.
They do not know the hidden things of God,
they have no hope that holiness will be rewarded,
they can see no reward for blameless souls.

This is the word of the Lord.

Responsorial Psalm Ps 33:16. 18. 19-21. 23. ℟ v.19

℟ The Lord is close to the broken-hearted.

1. The Lord turns his face against the wicked
   to destroy their remembrance from the earth.
   The just call and the Lord hears
   and rescues them in all their distress. ℟

2. The Lord is close to the broken-hearted;
   those whose spirit is crushed he will save.
   Many are the trials of the just man

but from them all the Lord will rescue him. ℟

3 He will keep guard over all his bones,
not one of his bones shall be broken.
The Lord ransoms the souls of his servants.
Those who hide in him shall not be condemned. ℟

Gospel Acclamation Joel 2:12-13
Praise to you, O Christ, king of eternal glory.
Now, now — it is the Lord who speaks —
come back to me with all your heart,
for I am all tenderness and compassion.
Praise to you, O Christ, king of eternal glory.

or   Mt 4:4

Praise to you, O Christ, king of eternal glory.
Man does not live on bread alone,
but on every word that comes from the mouth of God.
Praise to you, O Christ, king of eternal glory.

Gospel

A reading from the holy Gospel according to John
7:1-2.10.25-30
They would have arrested him, but his time had not yet come.

Jesus stayed in Galilee; he could not stay in Judaea, because the Jews were out to kill him.

As the Jewish feast of Tabrnacles drew near, after his brothers had left for the festival, Jesus went up as well, but quite privately, without drawing attention to himself.

Meanwhile some of the people of Jerusalem were saying, 'Isn't this the man they want to kill? And here he is, speaking freely, and they have nothing to say to him! Can it be true the authorities have made up their minds that he is the Christ? Yet we all know where he comes from, but when the Christ appears no one will know where he comes from.'

Then, as Jesus taught in the Temple, he cried out:

'Yes, you know me and you know where I came from.
Yet I have not come of myself;
no, there is one who sent me and I really come from him,
and you do not know him,
but I know him
because I have come from him
and it was he who sent me.'

They would have arrested him then, but because his time had not yet come no one laid a hand on him.

This is the Gospel of the Lord.

Prayer over the Gifts
All-powerful God,

may the healing power of this sacrifice
free us from sin
and help us to approach you with pure hearts.

Preface of Lent I-IV. (p.8)

Communion Antiphon
In Christ, through the shedding of his blood, we have redemption and forgiveness of our sins by the abundance of his grace.

Prayer after Communion
Lord,
in this eucharist we pass from death to life.
Keep us from our old and sinful ways
and help us to continue in the new life.

Solemn Blessing or Prayer over the People (p.20)

SATURDAY

Lord God, I take refuge in you. *It is difficult to come to faith. There are arguments for and against. Prejudice can blind, and ridicule and contempt can become weapons of self defence. Jeremiah meets all this, and sees himself as a lamb led to the slaughter. Jesus, the Lamb of God, suffers death for the blindness of many.*

Entrance Antiphon
The snares of death overtook me, the ropes of hell tightened around me; in my distress I called upon the Lord, and he heard my voice.

Opening Prayer
Lord,
guide us in your gentle mercy,
for left to ourselves
we cannot do your will.

Liturgy of the Word
First Reading

A reading from the prophet Jeremiah   11:18-20
I was like a trustful lamb being led to the slaughter-house.

The Lord revealed it to me; I was warned. Lord, that was when you opened my eyes to their scheming. I for my part was like a trustful lamb being led to the slaughter-house, not knowing the schemes they were plotting against me. Let us destroy the tree in its strength, let us cut him off from the land of the living, so that his name may be quickly forgotten!'

But you, Lord of hosts, who pronounce a just sentence,
who probe the loins and heart,
let me see the vengeance you will take on them,
for I have committed my cause to you.

This is the word of the Lord.

Responsorial Psalm Ps 7:2-3. 9-12.
℟ v.2

℟ **Lord God, I take refuge in you.**

1 Lord God, I take refuge in you.
  From my pursuer save me and rescue me,
  lest he tear me to pieces like a lion
  and drag me off with no one to rescue me. ℟

2 Give judgement for me, Lord; I am just
  and innocent of heart.
  Put an end to the evil of the wicked!
  Make the just stand firm, you who test mind and heart,
  O just God! ℟

3 God is the shield that protects me,
  who saves the upright of heart.
  God is a just judge slow to anger;
  but he threatens the wicked every day. ℟

Gospel Acclamation   *Ez 33:11*
  Praise and honour to you, Lord Jesus!
  I take pleasure, not in the death of a wicked man,
  — it is the Lord who speaks
  — but in the turning back of a wicked man
  who changes his ways to win life.
  Praise and honour to you, Lord Jesus!

or   *cf. Lk 8:15*

  Praise and honour to you, Lord Jesus!
  Blessed are those who,
  with a noble and generous heart,
  take the word of God to themselves
  and yield a harvest through their perseverance.
  Praise and honour to you, Lord Jesus!

Gospel

A reading from the holy Gospel according to John   7:40-52
Would the Christ be from Galilee?

Several people who had been listening to Jesus said, 'Surely he must be the prophet', and some said, 'He is the Christ', but others said, 'Would the Christ be from Galilee? Does not scripture say that the Christ must be descended from David and come from the town of Bethlehem?' So the people could not agree about him. Some would have liked to arrest him, but no one actually laid hands on him.

The police went back to the chief priests and Pharisees who said to them, 'Why haven't you brought him?' The police replied, 'There has never been anybody who has spoken like him.' 'So' the Pharisees answered 'you have been led astray as well? Have any of the authorities believed in him? Any of the Pharisees? This table knows nothing about the Law — they are damned.' One of them, Nicodemus — the same man who had come to Jesus earlier — said to them, 'But surely the Law does not allow us to pass judgement on a man without giving him a hearing and discovering what he is about?' To this they answered, 'Are you a Galilean too? Go into the matter, and see for yourself: prophets do not come out of Galilee.'

This the Gospel of the Lord.

Prayer over the Gifts
Father,
accept our gifts
and make our hearts obedient to your will.

Preface of Lent I-IV. p.8.

Communion Antiphon
We have been ransomed with the precious blood of Christ, as with the blood of a lamb without blemish or spot.

Prayer after Communion
Lord,
may the power of your holy gifts free us from sin
and help us to please you in our daily lives.

Solemn Blessing or Prayer over the People (p.20)

FIFTH WEEK OF LENT
MONDAY

If there is one of you who has not sinned, let him be the first to throw a stone. *The differences between Jesus and those who would condemn him are brought out each day this week. In the story of the woman taken in adultery Jesus shows that her accusers are in truth greater sinners. They judge by human standards but God judges differently. So also the accusers of Susanna are the real sinners before God. The Shepherd Lord who gives comfort in dark ways will be faithful to all who walk justly before him.*

Entrance Antiphon
God, take pity on me! My enemies are crushing me; all day long they wage war on me.

Opening Prayer
Father of love, source of all blessings,
help us to pass from our old life of sin
to the new life of grace.
Prepare us for the glory of your kingdom.

Liturgy of the Word
First Reading

A reading from the prophet Daniel
13:1-9, 15-17, 19-30, 33-62
Have I to die, innocent as I am?

In Babylon there lived a man named Joakim. He had married Susanna daughter of Hilkiah, a woman of great beauty; and she was God-fearing, because her parents were worthy people and had instructed their daughter in the Law of Moses. Joakim was a very rich man, and had a garden attached to his house; the Jews would often visit him since he was held in greater respect than any other man. Two elderly men had been selected from the people that year to act as judges. Of such the Lord said, 'Wickedness has come to Babylon through the elders and judges posing as guides to the people.' These men were often at Joakim's house, and all who were engaged in litigation used to come to them. At midday, when everyone had gone, Susanna used to take a walk in her husband's garden. The two elders, who used to watch her every day as she came in to take her walk, gradually began to desire her. They threw reason aside, making no effort to turn their eyes to heaven, and forgetting its demands of virtue. So they waited for a favourable moment; and one day Susanna came as usual, accompanied only by two young maidservants. The day was hot and she wanted to bathe in the garden. There was no one about except the two elders, spying on her from their hiding place. She said to the servants, 'Bring me some oil and balsam and shut the garden door while I bathe.'

Hardly were the servants gone than the two elders were there after her. 'Look,' they said 'the garden door is shut, no one can see. We want to have you, so give in and let us! Refuse, and we will both give evidence that a young man was with you and that was why you sent your maids away.'

Susanna sighed. 'I am trapped,' she said 'whatever I do. If I agree, that means my death, if I resist, I cannot get away from you. But I prefer to fall innocent into your power than to sin in the eyes of the Lord.' Then she cried out as loud as she could. The two elders began shouting too, putting the blame on her, and one of them ran to open the garden door. The household, hearing the shouting in the garden, rushed out by the side entrance to see what was happening; once the elders had told their story the servants were thoroughly taken aback, since nothing of this sort had ever been said of Susanna.

Next day a meeting was held at the house of her husband Joakim. The two elders arrived; in their vindictiveness determined to have her put to death. They addressed the company: 'Summon Susanna daughter of Hilkiah and wife of Joakim.' She was sent for, and came accompanied by her parents, her children and all her relations.

All her own people were weeping, and so were all the others who saw her. The two elders stood up, with all the people round them, and laid their hands on the woman's head. Tearfully she turned her eyes to heaven, her heart confident in God. The elders then spoke. 'While we were walking by ourselves in the garden, this woman arrived with two servants. She shut the garden door and then dismissed the servants. A young man who had been hiding went over to her and they lay down together. From the end of the garden where we were, we saw this crime taking place and hurried towards them. Though we saw them together we were unable to catch the man: he was too strong for us; he opened the door and took to his heels. We did, however, catch this woman and ask her who the young man was. She refused to tell us. That is our evidence.'

Since they were elders of the people, and judges, the assembly took their word: Susanna was condemned to death. She cried out as loud as she could, 'Eternal God, you know all secrets and everything before it happens; you know that they have given false evidence against me. And now have I to die, innocent as I am of everything their malice has invented against me?'

The Lord heard her cry and, as she was being led away to die, he roused the holy spirit residing in a young boy named Daniel who began to shout, 'I am innocent of this woman's death!' At which all the people turned to him and asked, 'What do you mean by these words?' Standing in the middle of the crowd he replied, 'Are you so stupid, sons of Israel, as to condemn a daughter of Israel unheard and without troubling to find out the truth? Go back to the scene of the trial: these men have given false evidence against her.'

All the people hurried back, and the elders said to Daniel, Come and sit with us and tell us what you mean, since God has given you the gifts that elders have.' Daniel said 'Keep the men well apart from each other for I want to question them.' When the men had been separated, Daniel had one of them brought to him. 'You have grown old in wickedness,' he said, 'and now the sins of your earlier days have overtaken you, you with your unjust judgements, your condemnation of the innocent, your acquittal of guilty men, when the Lord has said, "You must not put the innocent and the just to death." Now then, since you saw her so clearly, tell me what tree you saw them lying under?' He replied, 'Under a mastic tree.' Daniel said, 'True enough! Your lie recoils on your own head: the angel of God has already received your sentence from him and will slash you in half.' He dismissed the man, ordered the other to be brought and said to him, 'Spawn of Canaan, not of Judah, beauty has seduced you, lust has led your heart astray! This is how you have been behaving with the daughters of Israel and they were too frightened to resist; but here is a daughter of Judah who could not stomach your wickedness! Now then, tell me what tree you surprised them under?' He replied, 'Under a holm oak.' Daniel said, 'True enough! Your lie recoils on your own head: the angel of God is waiting, with a sword to drive home and split you, and destroy the pair of you.'

Then the whole assembly shouted, blessing God, the saviour of those who trust in him. And they turned on the two elders whom Daniel had convicted of false evidence out of their own mouths. As prescribed in the Law of Moses, they sentenced them to the same punishment as they had intended to inflict on their neighbour. They put them to death; the life of an innocent woman was spared that day.

This is the word of the Lord.

Responsorial Psalm   *Ps 22.* ℟ *v.4*
℟ **If I should walk in the valley of darkness
no evil would I fear.**

1 The Lord is my shepherd;
   there is nothing I shall want.
  Fresh and green are the pastures
   where he gives me repose.
  Near restful waters he leads me,
   to revive my drooping spirit. ℟

2 He guides me along the right path;
   he is true to his name.
  If I should walk in the valley of darkness
   no evil would I fear.
  You are there with your crook and your staff;
   with these you give me comfort. ℟

3 You have prepared a banquet for me
   in the sight of my foes.
  My head you have anointed with oil;
   my cup is overflowing. ℟

4 Surely goodness and kindness shall follow me
   all the days of my life.
  In the Lord's own house shall I dwell
   for ever and ever. ℟

Gospel Acclamation   *2 Cor 6:2*
  Glory to you, O Christ, you are the Word of God!
  Now is the favourable time;
  this is the day of salvation.
  Glory to you, O Christ, you are the Word of God!

or   *Ez 33:11*

  Glory to you, O Christ, you are the Word of God!
  I take pleasure, not in the death of a wicked man
   — it is the Lord who speaks —
  but in the turning back of a wicked man
  who changes his ways to win life.
  Glory to you, O Christ, you are the Word of God!

Gospel

A reading from the holy Gospel according to John   *8:1-11*
If there is one of you who has not sinned, let him be the first to throw a stone at her.

Jesus went to the Mount of Olives. At daybreak he appeared in the

Temple again; and as all the people came to him, he sat down and began to teach them.

The scribes and Pharisees brought a woman along who had been caught committing adultery; and making her stand there in full view of everybody, they said to Jesus, 'Master, this woman was caught in the very act of committing adultery, and Moses has ordered us in the Law to condemn women like this to death by stoning. What have you to say?' They asked him this as a test, looking for something to use against him. But Jesus bent down and started writing on the ground with his finger. As they persisted with their question, he looked up and said, 'If there is one of you who has not sinned, let him be the first to throw a stone at her.' Then he bent down and wrote on the ground again. When they heard this they went away one by one; beginning with the eldest, until Jesus was left alone with the woman, who remained standing there. He looked up and said, 'Woman, where are they? Has no one condemned you?' 'No one sir,' she replied. 'Neither do I condemn you,' said Jesus 'go away and don't sin any more.'

This is the Gospel of the Lord.

Alternative Gospel

For use in Year C when John 8:1-11 is read on the preceding Sunday.

A reading from the holy Gospel according to John   8:12-20
I am the light of the world.

Jesus said to the people:
> 'I am the light of the world;
> anyone who follows me will
>   not be walking in the
>   dark;
> he will have the light of life.'

At this the Pharisees said to him, 'You are testifying on your own behalf; your testimony is not valid.' Jesus replied:

> 'It is true that I am testifying
>   on my own behalf,
> but my testimony is still
>   valid,
> because I know
> where I came from and
>   where I am going;
> but you do not know
> where I come from or where
>   I am going.
> You judge by human
>   standards;
> I judge no one,
> but if I judge,
> my judgement will be sound,
> because I am not alone:
> the one who sent me is with
>   me;
> and in your Law it is written
> that the testimony of two
>   witnesses is valid.
> I may be testifying on my
>   own behalf,
> but the Father who sent me
>   is my witness too.'

They asked him, 'Where is your Father?' Jesus answered:

'You do not know me, nor do you know my Father; if you did know me, you would know my Father as well.'

He spoke these words in the Treasury, while teaching in the Temple. No one arrested him, because his time had not yet come.

This is the Gospel of the Lord.

Prayer over the Gifts
Lord,
as we come with joy
to celebrate the mystery of the eucharist,
may we offer you hearts
purified by bodily penance.

Preface of the Passion of the Lord I. (p.9)

Communion Antiphon
(When the gospel of the woman taken is adultery is read)
Has no one condemned you? The woman answered: No one, Lord. Neither do I condemn you: go and do not sin again.

or

When other gospels are read
I am the light of the world, says the Lord; the man who follows me will have the light of life.

Prayer after Communion
Father,
through the grace of your sacraments
may we follow Christ more faithfully
and come to the joy of your kingdom,
where he is Lord for ever and ever.

Solemn Blessing or Prayer over the People (p.20)

TUESDAY

If you do not believe that I am He, you will die in your sins. *Jesus raised up on the cross will become the sign of salvation for all people. To gaze with love upon the figure of Christ crucified has brought many from the ways of sin into the paths of holiness. For that cross is the sign of the depths of God's love for us.*

Entrance Antiphon
Put your hope in the Lord. Take courage and be strong.

Opening Prayer
Lord,
help us to do your will
that your Church may grow
and become more faithful in your service.

Liturgy of the Word
First Reading

A reading from the book of Numbers 21:4-9
If anyone is bitten and looks at the fiery serpent, he shall live.

The Israelites left Mount Hor by the road to the Sea of Suph, to skirt the land of Edom. On the way the people lost patience. They spoke against God and against Moses, 'Why did you bring us out of Egypt to die in this wilderness? For there is neither bread nor water here; we are sick of this unsatisfying food.'

At this God sent fiery serpents among the people; their bite brought death to many in Israel. The people came and said to Moses, 'We have sinned by speaking against the Lord and against you. Intercede for us with the Lord to save us from these serpents.' Moses interceded for the people, and the Lord answered him, 'Make a fiery serpent and put it on a standard. If anyone is bitten and looks at it, he shall live.' So Moses fashioned a bronze serpent which he put on a standard, and if anyone was bitten by a serpent, he looked at the bronze serpent and lived.

This is the word of the Lord.

Responsorial Psalm   *Ps 101:2-3. 16-21.* ℟ *v.2*

℟ **O Lord, listen to my prayer and let my cry for help reach you.**

1 O Lord, listen to my prayer
 and let my cry for help reach you.
 Do not hide your face from me
 in the day of my distress.
 Turn your ear towards me
 and answer me quickly when I call. ℟

2 The nations shall fear the name of the Lord
 and all the earth's kings your glory,
 when the Lord shall build up Zion again
 and appear in all his glory.
 Then he will turn to the prayers of the helpless;
 he will not despise their prayers. ℟

3 Let this be written for ages to come
 that a people yet unborn may praise the Lord;
 for the Lord leaned down from his sanctuary on high.
 He looked down from heaven to the earth
 that he might hear the groans of the prisoners
 and free those condemned to die. ℟

Gospel Acclamation   *Jn 8:12*
 Praise to you, O Christ, king of eternal glory!
 I am the light of the world, says the Lord,
 anyone who follows me will have the light of life.
 Praise to you, O Christ, king of eternal glory!

or

 Praise to you, O Christ, king of eternal glory!
 The seed is the word of God, Christ the sower;
 whoever finds this seed will remain for ever.

Praise to you, O Christ, king of eternal glory!

Gospel

A reading from the holy Gospel according to John   8:21-30
When you have lifted up the Son of Man, then you will know that I am He.

Jesus said to the Pharisees:
> 'I am going away; you will look for me
> and you will die in your sin.
> When I am going, you cannot come.'

The Jews said to one another, 'Will he kill himself? Is that what he means by saying, "Where I am going, you cannot come"?' Jesus went on:

> 'You are from below;
> I am from above.
> You are of this world;
> I am not of this world.
> I have told you already: You will die in your sins.
> Yes, if you do not believe that I am He,
> you will die in your sins.'

So they said to him, 'Who are you?' Jesus answered:

> 'What I have told you from the outset.
> About you I have much to say
> and much to condemn;
> but the one who sent me is truthful,
> and what I have learnt from him
> I declare to the world.'

They failed to understand that he was talking to them about the Father. So Jesus said:

> 'When you have lifted up the Son of Man,
> then you will know that I am He
> and that I do nothing of myself:
> what the Father has taught me
> is what I preach;
> he who sent me is with me,
> and has not left me to myself,
> for I always do what pleases him.'

As he was saying this, many came to believe in him.

This is the Gospel of Lord.

Prayer over the Gifts
Merciful Lord,
we offer this gift fo reconciliation
so that you will forgive our sins
and guide our wayward hearts.

Preface of the Passion of the Lord I. (p.9)

Communion Antiphon
When I am lifted up from the earth, I will draw all men to myself, says the Lord.

Prayer after Communion
All-powerful God,

may the holy mysteries we share in this eucharist
make us worthy to attain the gift of heaven.

Solemn Blessing or Prayer over the People (p.20)

WEDNESDAY

You will learn the truth and the truth will make you free. *Faith is personal: everyone has to be converted and discover the meaning of Jesus in their own lives. We cannot take for granted the inherited faith we have as members of the Church. Tested faith brings the blessing of God. We must keep searching for the truth that will make us free indeed.*

Entrance Antiphon
Lord, you rescue me from raging enemies, you lift me above my attackers, you deliver me from violent men.

Opening Prayer
Father of mercy,
hear the prayers of your repentant children
who call on you in love.
Enlighten our minds and sanctify our hearts.

Liturgy of the Word
First Reading

A reading from the prophet Daniel
3:14-20, 24-25, 28
He has sent his angel to rescue his servants.

King Nebuchadnezzar said, 'Shadrach, Meshach and Abednego, is it true that you do not serve my gods, and that you refuse to worship the golden statue I have erected? When you hear the sound of horn, pipe, lyre, trigon, harp, bagpipe, or any other instrument, are you prepared to prostrate yourselves and worship the statue I have made? If you refuse to worship it, you must be thrown straight away into the burning fiery furnace, and where is the god who could save you from my power?' Shadrach, Meshach and Abednego replied to King Nebuchadnezzar, 'You question hardly requires an answer: if our God, the one we serve is able to save us from the burning fiery furnace and from your power, O king, he will save us, and even if he does not, then you must know, O king, that we will not serve your god or worship the statue you have erected.' These words infuriated King Nebuchadnezzar; his expression was very different now as he looked at Shadrach, Meshach and Abednego. He gave orders for the furnace to be made seven times hotter than usual, and commanded certain stalwarts from his army to bind Shadrach Meshach and Abednego and throw them into the burning fiery furnace.

Then King Nebuchadnezzar sprang to his feet in amazement. He said to his advisers, 'Did we not have these three men thrown bound into the fire?' They replied, 'Certainly, O king.' 'But,' he went on 'I can see four men walking about freely in the heart of the fire without coming to any harm.' And the fourth looks like a son of the gods.'

Nebuchadnezzar exclaimed, 'Blessed be the God of Shadrach, Meshach and Abednego: he has sent his angel to rescue his servants who, putting their trust in him, defied the order of the king, and preferred to forfeit their bodies rather than serve or worship any god but their own.'

This is the word of the Lord.

Responsorial Psalm
    Dan 3:52-56. ℟ v.52
℟ **To you glory and praise for evermore.**

1 You are blest, Lord God of our fathers.
   Blest your glorious holy name. ℟

2 You are blest in the temple of your glory. You are blest on the throne of your kingdom. ℟

3 You are blest who gaze into the depths.
   ou are blest in the firmament of heaven. ℟

Gospel Acclamation   Mt 4:4
 Praise and honour to you, Lord Jesus!
 Man does not live on bread alone,
 but on every word that comes from the mouth of God.
 Praise and honour to you, Lord Jesus!

or   Lk 8:15

 Praise and honour to you, Lord Jesus!
 Blessed are those who,
 with a noble and generous heart,
 take the word of God to themselves
 and yield a harvest through their perseverance.
 Praise and honour to you, Lord Jesus!

Gospel

A reading from the holy Gospel according to John   8:31-42
If the Son of Man makes you free, you will be free indeed.

To the Jews who believed in him Jesus said:

 'If you make my word your home
 you will indeed be my disciples,
 you will learn the truth
 and the truth will make you free.'

They answered, 'We are descended from Abraham and we have never been the slaves of anyone; what do you mean, "You will be made free"?' Jesus replied:

 'I tell you most solemnly,
 everyone who commits sin is a slave.

> Now the slave's place in the house is not assured,
> but the son's place is assured.
> So if the Son makes you free, you will be free indeed.
> I know that you are descended from Abraham;
> but in spite of that you want to kill me
> because nothing I say has penetrated into you
> What I, for my part, speak of is what I have seen with my Father;
> but you, you put into action the lessons learnt from your father.'

They repeated, 'Our father is Abraham.' Jesus said to them:

> 'If you were Abraham's children,
> you would do as Abraham did.
> As it is, you want to kill me when I tell you the truth
> as I have learnt it from God;
> that is not what Abraham did.
> What you are doing is what your father does.'

'We were not born of prostitution,' they went on 'we have one father: God.' Jesus answered:

> 'If God were your father, you would love me,
> since I have come here from God; yes, I have come from him,
> not that I came because I chose,
> no, I was sent, and by him.'

> This is the Gospel of the Lord.

Prayer over the Gifts
Lord,
you have given us these gifts to honour your name.
Bless them,
and let them become a source of health and strength.

Preface of the Passion of the Lord I. (p.9)

Communion Antiphon
God has transferred us into the kingdom of the Son he loves; in him we are redeemed, and find forgiveness of our sins.

Prayer after Communion
Lord,
may the mysteries we receive heal us,
remove sin from our hearts,
and make us grow strong
under your constant protection.

Solemn Blessing or Prayer over the People (p.20)

THURSDAY

Before Abraham ever was, I AM.
The covenant of God with Abraham was the great glory of the people. Yet they forgot that they had responsibilities to live out that covenant. They are not in Jesus'

eyes true children of Abraham since they do not respect the covenant. When he tells them his relationship with Abraham they can only see a statement of blasphemy, and are further alienated. May we always remember the wonders God has done.

Entrance Antiphon
Christ is the mediator of a new covenant so that since he has died, those who are called may receive the eternal inheritance promised to them.

Opening Prayer
Lord,
come to us;
free us from the stain of our sins.
Help us to remain faithful to a holy way of life,
and guide us to the inheritance you have promised.

Liturgy of the Word
First Reading

A reading from the book of Genesis   17:3-9
You shall become the father of a multitude of nations.

Abram bowed to the ground and God said this to him. 'Here now is my covenant with you: you shall become the father of a multitude of nations. You shall no longer be called Abram; your name shall be Abraham, for I will make you father of a multitude of nations. I will make you most fruitful. I will make you into nations, and your issue shall be kings. I will establish my Covenant between myself and you, and your descendants after you, generation after generation, a Covenant in perpetuity, to be your God and the God of your descendants after you. I will give to you and to your descendants after you the land you are living in, the whole land of Canaan, to own in perpetuity, and I will be your God.'

God said to Abraham, 'You on your part shall maintain my Covenant, yourself and your descendants after you, generation after generation.'

This is the word of the Lord.

Responsorial Psalm   Ps 104:4-9.
                                   ℟ v.8
℟ **The Lord remembers his covenant for ever.**

1 Consider the Lord and his strength;
  constantly seek his face.
  Remember the wonders he has done,
  his miracles, the judgements he spoke. ℟

2 O children of Abraham, his servant,
  O sons of the Jacob he chose.
  He, the Lord, is our God;
  his judgements prevail in all the earth. ℟

3 He remembers his covenant for ever,

Fifth Week of Lent: Thursday

his promise for a thousand
    generations,
the covenant he made with
    Abraham,
the oath he swore to Isaac.

℟

Gospel Acclamation
cf. Jn 6:63-68

Glory and praise to you,
    O Christ!
Your words are spirit, Lord,
    and they are life;
you have the message of
    eternal life.
Glory and praise to you, O
    Christ!

or cf. Ps 94:8

Glory and praise to you, O
    Christ!
Harden not your hearts today
but listen to the voice of the
    Lord.
Glory and praise to you, O
    Christ!

Gospel

A reading from the holy Gospel according to John 8:51-59
Your father Abraham rejoiced to think that he would see my Day.

Jesus said to the Jews:

'I tell you most solemnly,
whoever keeps my word
will never see death.'

The Jews said, 'Now we know for certain that you are possessed. Abraham is dead, and the prophets are dead, and yet you say, "Whoever keeps my word will never know the taste of death." Are you greater than our father Abraham, who is dead? The prophets are dead too. Who are you claiming to be?' Jesus answered:

'If I were to seek my own
    glory
that would be no glory at all;
my glory is conferred by the
    Father,
by the one of whom you say,
    "He is our God"
although you do not know
    him,
But I know him,
and if I were to say: I do not
    know him,
I should be a liar, as you are
    liars yourselves.
But I do know him, and I
    faithfully keep his word.
Your father Abraham rejoiced
to think that he would see
    my Day;
he saw it and was glad.'

The Jews then said, 'You are not fifty yet, and you have seen Abraham!' Jesus replied:

'I tell you most solemnly,
before Abraham ever was,
I Am.'

At this they picked up stones to throw at him, but Jesus hid himself and left the Temple.

This is the Gospel of the Lord.

Prayer over the Gifts
Merciful Lord,
accept the sacrifice we offer you
that it may help us grow in holiness
and advance the salvation of the world.

Preface of the Passion of the Lord I. (p.9)

Communion Antiphon
God did not spare his own Son, but gave him up for us all; with Christ he will surely give us all things.

Prayer after Communion
Lord of mercy,
Let the sacrament which renews us bring us to eternal life.

Solemn Blessing or Prayer over the People (p.20)

FRIDAY

The Lord is at my side, a mighty hero. *Jeremiah in the face of misunderstanding, opposition and persecution still holds fast to his belief that God is at his side as a mighty hero. All prophets need this courage for they must face even death. Jesus recognises that the Father has consecrated him and sent him into the world. He knows that some at least will come to faith in him.*

Entrance Antiphon
Have mercy on me, Lord, for I am in distress, rescue me from the hands of my enemies. Lord, keep me from shame, for I have called to you.

Opening Prayer
Lord,
grant us your forgiveness,
and set us free from our enslavement to sin.

Liturgy of the Word
First Reading

A reading from the prophet Jeremiah   20:10-13
The Lord is at my side, a mighty hero.
Jeremiah said:
 I hear so many disparaging me,
 ' "Terror from every side!"
 Denounce him! Let us denounce him!'
 All those who used to be my friends
 watched for my downfall,
 "Perhaps he will be seduced into error.
 Then we will master him
 and take our revenge!"
 But the Lord is at my side, a mighty hero,
 my opponents will stumble, mastered,
 confounded by their failure;
 everlasting, unforgettable disgrace will be theirs.
 But you, Lord of hosts, you who probe with justice,
 who scrutinise the loins and heart,
 let me see the vengeance you will take on them,

for I have committed my
    cause to you.
Sing to the Lord,
praise the Lord,
for he has delivered the soul
    of the needy
from the hands of evil men.'

This is the word of the Lord.

Responsorial Psalm Ps 17:2-7.
℞ cf. v.7

℞ **In my anguish I called to the Lord
and he heard my voice.**

1 I love you, Lord, my
     strength,
   my rock, my fortress, my
     saviour.
   My God is the rock where I
     take refuge;
   my shield, my mighty help,
     my stronghold.
   The Lord is worthy of all
     praise:
   when I call I am saved from
     my foes. ℞

2 The waves of death rose
     about me;
   the torrents of destruction
     assailed me;
   the snares of the grave
     entangled me;
   the traps of death confronted
     me. ℞

3 In my anguish I called to the
     Lord;
   I cried to my God for help.
   From his temple he heard my
     voice;
   my cry came to his ears. ℞

Gospel Acclamation Mt 4:17
   Glory to you, O Christ, you
     are the Word of God!
   Repent, says the Lord,
   for the kingdom of heaven is
     close at hand.
   Glory to you, O Christ, you
     are the Word of God!

or cf. Jn 6:63-68

   Glory to you, O Christ, you
     are the Word of God!
   Your words are spirit, Lord,
     and they are life;
   you have the message of
     eternal life.
   Glory to you, O Christ, you
     are the Word of God!

Gospel

A reading from the holy Gospel
according to John 10:31-42
*They wanted to arrest Jesus then,
but he eluded them.*

The Jews fetched stones to stone him, so Jesus said to them, 'I have done many good works for you to see, works from my Father; for which of these are you stoning me?' The Jews answered him, 'We are not stoning you for doing a good work but for blasphemy: you are only a man and you claim to be God.' Jesus answered:

   'Is it not written in your Law:
   I said, you are gods?
   So the Law used the word
     gods
   of those to whom the word
     of God was addressed,

and scripture cannot be
   rejected.
Yet you say to someone the
   Father has consecrated
   and sent into the world,
"You are blaspheming,"
because he says, "I am the
   Son of God."
If I am not doing my Father's
   work,
there is no need to believe
   me;
but if I am doing it,
then even if you refuse to
   believe in me,
at least believe in the work I
   do;
then you will know for sure
that the Father is in me and I
   am in the Father.'

Then wanted to arrest him then, but he eluded them.

He went back again to the far side of the Jordan to stay in the district where John had once been baptising. Many people who came to him there said, 'John gave no signs, but all he said about this man was true'; and many of them believed in him.

This is the Gospel of the Lord.

Prayer over the Gifts
God of mercy,
may the gifts we present at your
   altar
help us to achieve eternal
   salvation.

Preface of the Passion of the Lord I. (p.9)

Communion Antiphon
Jesus carried our sins in his own body on the cross so that we could die to sin and live in holiness; by his wounds we have been healed.

Prayer after Communion
Lord,
may we always receive the protection of this sacrifice.
May it keep us safe from all harm.

Solemn Blessing or Prayer over the People (p.20)

SATURDAY

Jesus was to die to gather together in unity the scattered children of God. *Ezechiel foreshadows the final unity of the children of God. Jesus is the one who will die to gather together in unity the scattered children of God. By his death he has made all one, reconciling all humankind with God.*

Entrance Antiphon
Lord, do not stay away; come quickly to help me! I am a worm and no man: men scorn me, people despise me.

Opening Prayer
God our Father,
you always work to save us,
and now we rejoice in the great
   love
you give to your chosen people.

Protect all who are about to become your children,
and continue to bless those who are already baptised.

Liturgy of the Word
First Reading

A reading from the prophet Ezekiel 37:21-28

I will make them into one nation.

This Lord says this: 'I am going to take the sons of Israel from the nations where they have gone. I shall gather them together from everywhere and bring them home to their own soil. I shall make them into one nation in my own land and on the mountains of Israel, and one king is to be king of them all; they will no longer form two nations, nor be two separate kingdoms. They will no longer defile themselves with their idols and their filthy practices and all their sins. I shall rescue them from all the betrayals they have been guilty of; I shall cleanse them; they shall be my people and I will be their God. My servant David will reign over them, one shepherd for all; they will follow my observances, respect my laws and practise them. They will live in the land that I gave my servant Jacob, the land in which your ancestors lived. They will live in it, they, their children, their children's children, for ever. David my servant is to be their prince for ever. I shall make a covenant of peace with them, an eternal covenant with them. I shall resettle them and increase them; I shall settle my sanctuary among them for ever. I shall make my home above them, I will be their God, they shall be my people. And the nations will learn that I am the Lord the sanctifier of Israel, when my sanctuary is with them for ever.'

This is the word of the Lord.

Responsorial Psalm
Jer 31:10-13. ℟ v.10

℟ **The Lord will guard us as a shepherd guards his flock.**

1. O nations, hear the word of the Lord,
proclaim it to the far-off coasts.
Say: 'He who scattered Israel will gather him
and guard him as a shepherd guards his flock.' ℟

2. For the Lord has ransomed Jacob,
has saved him from an overpowering hand.
They will come and shout for joy on Mount Zion,
they will stream to the blessings of the Lord. ℟

3. Then the young girls will rejoice and will dance,
the men, young and old, will be glad.
I will turn their mourning into joy.
I will console them, give gladness for grief. ℟

Gospel Acclamation Jn 3:16
> Praise to you, O Christ, king of eternal glory!
> God loved the world so much that he gave his only Son;
> everyone who believes in him has eternal life.
> Praise to you, O Christ, king of eternal glory!

or Ez 18:31
> Praise to you, O Christ, king of eternal glory!
> Shake off all your sins — it is the Lord who speaks —
> and make yourselves a new heart and a new spirit.
> Praise to you, O Christ, king of eternal glory!

Gospel

A reading from the holy Gospel according to John 11:45-56
To gather together in unity the scattered children of God.

Many of the Jews who had come to visit Mary and had seen what Jesus did believed in him, but some of them went to tell the Pharisees what he had done. Then the chief priests and Pharisees called a meeting. 'Here is this man working all these signs' they said 'and what action are we taking? If we let him go on in this way everybody will believe in him, and the Romans will come and destroy the Holy Place and our nation.' One of them, Caiaphas, the high priest that year, said, 'You don't seem to have grasped the situation at all, you fail to see that it is better for one man to die for the people, than for the whole nation to be destroyed.' He did not speak in his own person, it was as high priest that he made this prophecy that Jesus was to die for the nation — and not for the nation only, but to gather together in unity the scattered children of God. From that day they were determined to kill him. So Jesus no longer went about openly among the Jews, but left the district for a town called Ephraim, in the country bordering on the desert, and stayed there with his disciples.

The Jewish Passover drew near, and many of the country people who had gone up to Jerusalem to purify themselves looked out for Jesus, saying to one another as they stood about in the Temple, 'What do you think? Will he come to the festival or not?'

This is the Gospel of the Lord.

Prayer over the Gifts
Ever-living God,
in baptism, the sacrament of our faith,
you restore us to life.
Accept the prayers and gifts of your people:
forgive our sins and fulfil our hopes and desires.

Preface of the Passion of the Lord I. (p.9)

Communion Antiphon
Christ was sacrificed so that he could gather together the scattered children of God.

Prayer after Communion
Father of mercy and power,
we thank you for nourishing us with the body and blood of Christ
and for calling us to share in his divine life,
for he is Lord for ever and ever.

Solemn Blessing or Prayer over the People (p.20)

HOLY WEEK

MONDAY

He does not break the crushed reed, nor quench the wavering flame. *The scripture readings today focus on the coming Passion of Jesus Christ. The Servant Songs from Isaiah describe an individual, who is also the people whom he represents. He is realised in Jesus, the one who suffers for his people. The Gospel shows us how even in this scene of family life the actions of Jesus divide people into those who are for him and those who oppose him. In the psalm we pray with Jesus, and with all who suffer opposition, for the support of the Lord God.*

Entrance Antiphon
Defend me, Lord, from all my foes: take up your arms and come swiftly to my aid for you have the power to save me.

Opening Prayer
All-powerful God,
by the suffering and death of your Son,
strengthen and protect us in our weakness.

Liturgy of the Word
First Reading

A reading from the prophet Isaiah
42:1-7
He does not cry out or shout aloud.

> Here is my servant whom I uphold,
> my chosen one in whom my soul delights.
> I have endowed him with my spirit
> that he may bring true justice to the nations.
>
> He does not cry out or shout aloud,
> or make his voice heard in the streets.
> He does not break the crushed reed,
> nor quench the wavering flame.
>
> Faithfully he brings true justice;
> he will neither waver, nor be crushed
> until true justice is established on earth,
> for the islands are awaiting his law.

Thus says God, the Lord,
he who created the heavens
    and spread them out,
who gave shape to the earth
    and what comes from it,
who gave breath to its
    people
and life to the creatures that
    move in it:

I, the Lord, have called you
    to serve the cause of right;
I have taken you by the
    hand and formed you;
I have appointed you as
    covenant of the people
    and light of the nations,
to open the eyes of the
    blind,
to free captives from prison,
and those who live in
    darkness from the
    dungeon.

This is the word of the Lord.

*Responsorial Psalm   Ps 26:1-3,
                13-14.* ℟ *v.1*

℟ **The Lord is my light and my help.**

1 The Lord is my light and my
        help;
    whom shall I fear?
    The Lord is the stronghold of
        my life;
    before whom shall I shrink? ℟

2 When evil-doers draw near
        to devour my flesh,
    it is they, my enemies and
        foes,
    who stumble and fall. ℟

3 Though an army encamp
        against me
    my heart would not fear.
    Though war break out
        against me
    even then would I trust. ℟

4 I am sure I shall see the
        Lord's goodness
    in the land of the living.
    Hope in him, hold firm and
        take heart.
    Hope in the Lord! ℟

Gospel Acclamation
    Praise and honour to you,
        Lord Jesus!
    Hail to you, our King!
    You alone have had
        compassion on our sins.
    Praise and honour to you,
        Lord Jesus!

Gospel

A reading from the holy Gospel according to John   *12:1-11*
Leave her alone; she had to keep this scent for the day of my burial.

Six days before the Passover, Jesus sent to Bethany, where Lazarus was, whom he had raised from the dead. They gave a dinner for him there; Martha waited on them and Lazarus was among those at table. Mary brought in a pound of very costly ointment, pure nard, and with it anointed the feet of Jesus, wiping them with her hair; the house was full of the scent of the ointment. Then Judas Iscariot — one of his disciples, the man who was to betray him — said, 'Why wasn't this ointment sold for three hundred denarii, and the money given to the poor?' He said this, not because he cared about the poor, but because he was a thief; he was in charge of the common fund and used to help himself to the contributions. So Jesus said, 'Leave her alone; she had to keep this scent for the day of my burial. You have the poor with you always, you will not always have me.'

Meanwhile a large number of Jews heard that he wdas there and came not only on account of Jesus but also to see Lazarus whom he had raised from the dead. Then the chief priests decided to kill Lazarus as well, since it was on his account that many of the Jews were leaving them and believing in Jesus.

This is the Gospel of the Lord.

Prayer over the Gifts
Lord,
look with mercy on our offerings.
May the sacrifice of Christ, your Son,
bring us to eternal life,
for he is Lord for ever and ever.

Preface of the Passion of the Lord I. (p.9)

Communion Antiphon
When I am in trouble, Lord, do not hide your face from me; hear me when I call, and answer me quickly.

Prayer after Communion
God of mercy,
be close to your people.
Watch over us who receive this sacrament of salvation,
and keep us in your love.

Solemn Blessing or Prayer over the People (p.20)

TUESDAY

I will make you the light of the nations. *The Suffering Servant is told that his mission is for all peoples, so he must not be disappointed at seeming failure now. In the Gospel we face the reality that some, like Judas, will totally reject God's offer of love. The psalm is Jesus' prayer for God's protection, we can pray it with him and with all who suffer persecution.*

Entrance Antiphon
False witnesses have stood up against me, and my enemies threaten violence; Lord, do not surrender me into their power!

Opening Prayer
Father,
may we receive your forgiveness and mercy
as we celebrate the passion and death of the Lord,
who lives and reigns. . . .

Liturgy of the Word
First Reading

A reading from the prophet Isaiah
49:1-6
I will make you the light of the nations so that my salvation may reach to the ends of the earth.

Islands, listen to me,
pay attention, remotest peoples.
The Lord called me before I was born,
from my mother's womb he pronounced my name.

He made my mouth a sharp sword,
and hid me in the shadows of his hand.
He made me into a sharpened arrow,
and concealed me in his quiver.

He said to me, 'You are my servant Israel,
in whom I shall be glorified';
while I was thinking, 'I have toiled in vain,
I have exhausted myself for nothing';

and all the while my cause was with the Lord,
my reward with my God.
I was honoured in the eyes of the Lord,
my God was my strength.

And now the Lord has spoken,
he who formed me in the womb to be his servant,
to bring Jacob back to him,
to gather Israel to him:

'It is not enough for you to be my servant,
to restore the tribes of Jacob and bring back the survivors of Israel;
I will make you the light of the nations
so that my salvation may reach to the ends of the earth.'

This is the word of the Lord.

Responsorial Psalm Ps 70:1-6, 15, 17. ℟ v.15

℟ **My lips will tell of your help.**

1 In you, O Lord, I take refuge;
let me never be put to shame.
In your justice rescue me, free me:
pay heed to me and save me. ℟

2 Be a rock where I can take refuge,
a mighty stronghold to save me;
for you are my rock, my stronghold.
Free me from the hand of the wicked. ℟

3 It is you, O Lord, who are my hope,
my trust, O Lord, since my youth.
On you I have leaned from my birth,
from my mother's womb you have been my help. ℟

4 My lips will tell of your justice
and day by day of your help
(though I can never tell it all).
O God, you have taught me from my youth
and I proclaim your wonders still. ℟

Holy Week: Tuesday

Gospel Acclamation
>Glory and praise to you, O Christ!
>Hail to you, our King!
>Obedient to the Father, you were led to your crucifixion
>as a meek lamb is led to the slaughter.
>Glory and praise to you, O Christ!

Gospel

A reading from the holy Gospel according to John   *13:21-33, 36-38*

One of you will betray me; before the cock crows, you will have disowned me three times.

While at supper with his disciples, Jesus was troubled in spirit and declared, 'I tell you most solemnly, one of you will betray me.' The disciples looked at one another, wondering which he meant. The disciple Jesus loved was reclining next to Jesus, Simon Peter signed to him and said, 'Ask who it is he means', so leaning back on Jesus' breast he said, 'Who is it, Lord?' 'It is the one' replied Jesus 'to whom I give the piece of bread that I shall dip in the dish.' He dipped the piece of bread and gave it to Judas son of Simon Iscariot. At that instant, after Judas had taken the bread, Satan entered him. Jesus then said, 'What you are going to do, do quickly.' None of the others at table understood the reason he said this. Since Judas had charge of the common fund, some of them though Jesus was telling him, 'Buy what we need for the festival', or telling him to give something to the poor. As soon as Judas had taken the piece of bread he went out. Night had fallen.

When he had gone Jesus said:

>'Now has the Son of Man been glorified,
>and in him God has been glorified.
>If God has been glorified in him,
>God will in turn glorify him in himself,
>and will glorify him very soon.
>My little children.
>I shall not be with you much longer.
>You will look for me,
>and, as I told the Jews,
>where I am going,
>you cannot come.'

Simon Peter said, 'Lord, where are you going?' Jesus replied, 'Where I am going you cannot follow me now; you will follow me later.' Peter said to him, 'Why can't I follow you now? I will lay down my life for you.' 'Lay down your life for me?' answered Jesus. 'I tell you most solemnly, before the cock crows you will have disowned me three times.'

This is the Gospel of the Lord.

Prayer over the Gifts
Lord,
look with mercy on our offerings.

May we who share the holy gifts
receive the life they promise.

Preface of the Passion of the Lord II. (p.9)

Communion Antiphon
God did not spare his own Son,
but gave him up for us all.

Prayer after Communion
God of mercy,
may the sacrament of salvation
which now renews our strength
bring us a share in your life for ever.

Solemn Blessing or Prayer over the People (p.20)

WEDNESDAY

The Son of Man is going to his fate, alas for that man by whom he is betrayed. *Because he is faithful to his mission the servant will undergo suffering: but he will survive because he listens to the Lord. Jesus suffers betrayal during the meal that symbolises liberation for all others. In the psalm the one who suffers for God's sake still has strength to praise him: we pray it for all who are judged or imprisoned unjustly.*

Entrance Antiphon
At the name of Jesus every knee must bend, in heaven, on earth, and under the earth; Christ became obedient for us even to death, dying on the cross. Therefore, to the glory of God the Father: Jesus Christ is Lord.

Opening Prayer
Father,
in your plan of salvation
your Son Jesus Christ accepted the cross
and freed us from the power of the enemy.
May we come to share the glory of his resurrection,
for he lives and reigns. . . .

Liturgy of the Word
First Reading

A reading from the prophet
Isaiah   50:4-9
I did not cover my face against insult and spittle.

> The Lord has given me
> a disciple's tongue.
> So that I may know how to reply to the wearied
> he provides me with speech.
> Each morning he wakes me to hear,
> to listen like a disciple.
> The Lord has opened my ear.
> For my part, I made no resistance,
> neither did I turn away.
> I offered my back to those who struck me,
> my cheeks to those who tore at my beard;
> I did not cover my face
> against insult and spittle.
> The Lord comes to my help,
> so that I am untouched by the insults.

So, too, I set my face like
   flint;
I know I shall not be
   shamed.
My vindicator is here at
   hand. Does anyone start
   proceedings against me?
Then let us go to court
   together.
Who thinks he has a case
   against me?
Let him approach me.
The Lord is coming to my
   help,
who dare condemn me?

This is the word of the Lord.

Responsional Psalm   Ps 68:8-10.
   21-22. 31. 33-34. ℟ v.14
℟ **In your great love, O Lord,
answer my prayer for your
favour.**

1 It is for you that I suffer
   taunts,
   that shame covers my face,
   that I have become a
      stranger to my brothers,
   an alien to my own mother's
      sons.
   I burn with zeal for your
      house
   and taunts against you fall on
      me. ℟

2 Taunts have broken my
   heart;
   I have reached the end of
      my strength.
   I looked in vain for
      compassion,
   for consolers; not one could
      I find.
   For food they gave me
      poison;
   in my thirst they gave me
      vinegar to drink. ℟

3 I will praise God's name with
      a song;
   I will glorify him with
      thanksgiving.
   The poor when they see it
      will be glad
   and God-seeking hearts will
      revive;
   for the Lord listens to the
      needy
   and does not spurn his
      servants in their chains. ℟

Gospel Acclamation
   Glory to you, O Christ, you
      are the Word of God!
   Hail to you, our King!
   Obedient to the Father, you
      were led to your
      crucifixion
   as a meek lamb is led to the
      slaughter.
   Glory to you, O Christ, you
      are the Word of God!

or

   Glory to you, O Christ, you
      are the Word of God!
   Hail to you, our King!
   You alone, have had
      compassion on our sins.
   Glory to you, O Christ, you
      are the Word of God!

Gospel
A reading from the holy Gospel
according to Matthew   26:14-25
The Son of Man is going to his fate,

as the scriptures say he will, but alas for that man by whom he is betrayed.

One of the Twelve, the man called Judas Iscariot, went to the chief priests and said, 'What are you prepared to give me if I hand him over to you?' They paid him thirty silver pieces, and from that moment he looked for an opportunity to betray him.

Now on the first day of Unleavened Bread the disciples came to Jesus to say, 'Where do you want us to make the preparations for you to eat the passover?' 'Go to so-and-so in the city' he replied 'and say to him, "The Master says: My time is near. It is at your house that I am keeping Passover with my disciples."' The disciples did what Jesus told them and prepared the Passover.

When evening came he was at table with the twelve disciples. And while they were eating he said, 'I tell you solemnly, one of you is about to betray me.' They were greatly distressed and started asking him in turn, 'Not I, Lord, surely?' He answered, 'Someone who has dipped his hand into the dish with me, will betray me. The Son of Man is going to his fate, as the scriptures say he will, but alas for that man by whom the Son of Man is betrayed! Better for that man if he had never been born!' Judas, who was to betray him, asked in his turn, 'Not I, Rabbi surely?' 'They are your own words' answered Jesus.

This is the Gospel of the Lord.

Prayer over the Gifts
Lord,
accept the gifts we present
as we celebrate this mystery
of the suffering and death of
 your Son.
May we share in the eternal life
 he won for us,
for he is Lord for ever and ever.

*Preface of the Passion of the
 Lord II. (p.9)*

Communion Antiphon
The Son of Man did not come to be served, but to serve, and to give his life as a ransom for many.

Prayer after Communion
All-powerful God,
the eucharist proclaims the death
 of your Son.
Increase our faith in its saving
 power
and strengthen our hope in the life
 it promises.

*Solemn Blessing or Prayer over the
 People (p.20)*

PROPER OF SAINTS

FEBRUARY

8 February
St Jerome Emiliani

Opening Prayer
God of mercy,
you chose Jerome Emiliani
to be a father and friend of
    orphans:
May his prayers keep us faithful
to the Spirit we have received,
who makes us your children.

Grant this through our Lord
    Jesus Christ, your Son,
who lives and reigns with you
    and the Holy Spirit,
one God, for ever and ever.

10 February
St Scholastica, virgin

Opening Prayer
Lord,
as we recall the memory of
    Saint Scholastica,
we ask that by her example
we may serve you with love
    and obtain perfect joy.

Grant this through our Lord
    Jesus Christ, your Son,
who lives and reigns with you
    and the Holy Spirit,
one God, for ever and ever.

11 February
Our Lady of Lourdes

Opening Prayer
God of mercy,
we celebrate the feast of Mary,
the sinless mother of God.
May her prayers help us
to rise above our human
    weakness.

We ask this through our Lord
    Jesus Christ, your Son,
who lives and reigns with you
    and the Holy Spirit,
one God, for ever and ever.

14 February
Ss Cyril, monk, and Methodius, bishop

Entrance Antiphon
The Lord chose these holy men for their unfeigned love, and gave them eternal glory. The Church has light by their teaching.

Opening Prayer
Father,
you brought the light of the
    gospel to the Slavic nations
through Saint Cyril and his
    brother Saint Methodius.
Open our hearts to understand
    your teaching
and help us to become one in
    faith and praise.

Liturgy of the Word
First Reading

A reading from the Acts of the Apostles 13:46-49

We must turn to the pagans.

Paul and Barnabas spoke out boldly to the Jews, 'We had to proclaim the word of God to your first, but since you have rejected it since you do not think yourselves worthy of eternal life, we must turn to the pagans. For this is what the Lord commanded us to do when he said:

'I have made you a light for the nations,
so that my salvation may reach the ends of the earth.'

It made the pagans very happy to hear this and they thanked the Lord for his message; all who were destined for eternal life became believers. Thus the word of the Lord spread through the whole countryside.

This is the word of the Lord.

Responsorial Psalm Ps 116.
℟ Mk 16:15

℟ **Go out to the whole world; proclaim the Good News.**

or

℟ **Alleluia!**
O praise the Lord, all you nations,
acclaim him all you peoples!
℟

Strong is his love for us,
he is faithful for ever. ℟

Gospel Acclamation Lk 4:18
Alleluia, alleluia!
The Lord has sent me to bring the good news to the poor,
to proclaim liberty to captives.
Alleluia!

Gospel

A reading from the holy Gospel according to Luke 10:1-9

The harvest is rich but the labourers are few.

The Lord appointed seventy-two others and sent them out ahead of him, in pairs, to all the towns and places he himself was to be. He said to them, 'The harvest is rich but the labourers are few, so ask the Lord of the harvest to send labourers to the harvest. Start off now, but remember, I am sending you out like lambs among wolves. Carry no purse, no haversack, no sandels. Salute no one on the road. Whatever house you go into, let your first words be, "Peace to this house!" And if a man of peace lives there, your peace will go and rest on him, if not, it will come back to you. Stay in the same house, taking what food and drink they have to offer, for the labourer deserves his wages; do not move from house to house. Whenever you go into a town where they make you welcome, eat what is set before you. Cure those men who are sick and say, "The kingdom of God is very near to you.'"

This is the Gospel of the Lord.

Prayer over the Gifts
Lord,
accept the gifts your people bring
on this feast of Saints Cyril and Methodius.
Give us purity of heart
and make us pleasing to you.

PREFACE OF HOLY MEN AND WOMEN II

Father, all-powerful and ever-living God,
we do well always and everywhere to give you thanks.

You renew the Church in every age
by raising up men and women outstanding in holiness,
living witnesses of your unchanging love.
They inspire us by their heroic lives,
and help us by their constant prayers
to be the living sign of your saving power.

We praise you, Lord, with all the angels and saints in their song of joy:

Holy, holy, holy. . .

Communion Antiphon
No longer shall I call you servants, for a servant knows not what his master does. Now I shall call you friends, for I have revealed to you all that I have heard from my Father.

Prayer after Communion
Lord,
as we share in your gifts,
we celebrate this feast of Saints Cyril and Methodius.
We honour the beginnings of our faith
and proclaim your glory in the saints.
May the salvation we receive from your altar
be our unending joy.

Solemn Blessing or Prayer over the People (p.20)

17 February

The Seven Founders of the Order of Servites

Opening Prayer
Lord,
fill us with the love
which inspired the seven holy brothers
to honour the Mother of God with special devotion
and to lead your people to you.

We ask this through our Lord Jesus Christ, your Son,
who lives and reigns with you and the Holy Spirit,
one God, for ever and ever.

21 February

St Peter Damian, bishop and doctor of the Church

Opening Prayer
All-powerful God,
help us to follow the teachings
    and example of Peter
    Damian.
By making Christ and the
    service of his Church
the first love of our lives,
may we come to the joys of
    eternal light,
where he lives and reigns with
    you and the Holy Spirit,
one God, for ever and ever.

22 February

The Chair of St Peter, Apostle

Entrance Antiphon
The Lord said to Simon Peter: I have prayed that your faith may not fail; and you in your turn must strengthen your brothers.

Opening Prayer
All-powerful Father,
you have built your Church
on the rock of Saint Peter's
    confession of faith.
May nothing divide or weaken
our unity in faith and love.

Grant this through our Lord
    Jesus Christ, your Son,
who lives and reigns with you
    and the Holy Spirit,
one God, for ever and ever.

Liturgy of the Word
First Reading

A reading from the first letter of St Peter 5:1-4
I am an elder myself and a witness to the sufferings of Christ.

I have something to tell your elders: I am an elder myself, and a witness to the sufferings of Christ, and with you I have a share in the glory that is to be revealed. Be the shepherds of the flock of God that is entrusted to you: watch over it, not simply as a duty but gladly, because God wants it; not for sordid money, but because you are eager to do it. Never be a dictator over any group that is put in your charge, but be an example that the whole flock can follow. When the chief shepherd appears, you will be given the crown of unfading glory.

This is the word of the Lord.

Responsorial Psalm Ps 22. ℟ v.1
℟ **The Lord is my shepherd; there is nothing I shall want.**

1 The Lord is my shepherd;
   there is nothing I shall want.
   Fresh and green are the
       pastures
   where he gives me repose.
   Near restful waters he leads
       me,
   to revive my drooping spirit.
                                ℟

2 He guides me along the right
   path;

he is true to his name.
If I should walk in the valley of darkness
no evil would I fear.
You are there with your crook and your staff,
with these you give me comfort. ℟

3 You have prepared a banquet for me
in the sight of my foes.
My head you have anointed with oil;
my cup is overflowing. ℟

4 Surely goodness and kindness shall follow me
all the days of my life.
In the Lord's own house shall I dwell
for ever and ever. ℟

Gospel Acclamation   Mt 16:18
Alleluia, alleluia!
You are Peter, and on this rock
I will build my Church.
And the gates of the underworld
can never hold out against it.
Alleluia!

Gospel

A reading from the holy Gospel according to Matthew   *16:13-19*
You are Peter, and I will give you the keys of the kingdom of heaven.

When Jesus came to the region of Caesarea Philippi he put the question to his disciples, 'Who do people say the Son of Man is'. And they said, 'Some say he is John the Baptist, some Elijah, and others Jeremiah or one of the prophets.' 'But you,' he said, 'who do you say I am?' They Simon Peter spoke up, 'You are the Christ,' he said, 'the Son of the living God.' Jesus replied, 'Simon son of Jonah, you are a happy man! Because it was not flesh and blood that revealed this to you but my Father in heaven. So I now say to you: You are Peter and on this rock I will build my Church. And the gates of the underworld can never hold out against it. I will give you the keys of the kingdom of heaven: whatever you bind on earth shall be considered bound in heaven: whatever you loose on earth shall be considered loosed in heaven.'

Prayer over the Gifts
Lord,
accept the prayers and gifts of your Church.
With Saint Peter as our shepherd,
keep us true to the faith he taught
and bring us to your eternal kingdom.

We ask this through Christ our Lord.

PREFACE OF THE APOSTLES I
Father, all-powerful and ever-living God,
we do well always and everywhere to give you thanks.

You are the eternal Shepherd
who never leaves his flock
   untended.
Through the apostles
you watch over us and protect
   us always.
You made them shepherds of
   the flock
to share in the work of your
   Son,
and from their place in heaven
   they guide us still.

And so, with all the choirs of
   angels in heaven
we proclaim your glory
and join in their unending hymn
   of praise.

Holy, holy, holy. . .

Communion Antiphon
                    Mt 16:16. 18
Peter said: 'You are the Christ, the Son of the Living God.' Jesus answered: 'You are Peter, the rock on which I will build my Church.'

Prayer after Communion
God our Father,
you have given us the body and
   blood of Christ
as the food of life.
On this feast of Peter the
   apostle,
may this communion bring us
   redemption
and be the sign and source of
   our unity and peace.

We ask this in the name of
   Jesus the Lord.

Solemn Blessing or Prayer over the People (p.20)

23 February
St Polycarp, bishop and martyr

Opening Prayer
God of all creation,
you gave your bishop Polycarp
the privilege of being counted
   among the saints
who gave their lives in faithful
   witness to the gospel.
May his prayers give us the
   courage
to share with him the cup of
   suffering
and to rise to eternal glory.

We ask this through our Lord
   Jesus Christ, your Son,
who lives and reigns with you
   and the Holy Spirit,
one God, for ever and ever.

MARCH
1 March
St David, bishop, patron of Wales

Entrance Antiphon   Isaiah 59:21; 56:7
My teaching, which I have put in your mouth, will never fail, says the Lord; the gifts which you offered on my altar will be accepted.

or

                    Psalm 15:5-6
You, Lord, are my portion and cup, you restore my inheritance to me; the way of life you marked out

for me has made my heritage glorious.

Opening Prayer
God our Father,
you gave the bishop David to the Welsh Church
to uphold the faith
and to be an example of Christian perfection.
In this changing world
may he help us to hold fast to the values
which bring eternal life.

Liturgy of the Word
First Reading

A reading from the letter of St Paul to the Philippians 3:8-14
I am racing for the finish, for the prize to which God calls us upwards to receive in Christ Jesus.

I believe nothing can happen that will outweigh the supreme advantage of knowing Christ Jesus my Lord. For him I have accepted the loss of everything, and I look on everything as so much rubbish if only I can have Christ and be given a place in him. I am no longer trying for perfection by my own efforts, the perfection that comes from the Law, but I want only the perfection that comes through faith in Christ, and is from God and based on faith. All I want is to know Christ and the power of his resurrection and to share his sufferings by reproducing the pattern of his death. That is the way I can hope to take my place in the resurrection of the dead. Not that I have become perfect yet: I have not yet won, but I am still running, trying to capture the prize for which Christ Jesus captured me. I can assure you my brothers, I am far from thinking that I have already won. All I can say is that I forget the past and I strain ahead for what is still to come; I am racing for the finish, for the prize to which God calls us upwards to receive in Christ Jesus.

This is the word of the Lord.

Responsorial Psalm Ps 1:1-4. 6
℟ **Happy the man who has placed his trust in the Lord.**

1 Happy indeed is the man
    who follows not the counsel of the wicked,
  nor lingers in the way of sinners
  nor sits in the company of scorners,
  but whose delight is the law of the Lord
  and who ponders his law day and night. ℟

2 He is like a tree that is planted
  beside the flowing waters,
  that yields its fruit in due season
  and whose leaves shall never fade;
  and all that he does shall prosper. ℟

3 Not so are the wicked, not so!
For they like winnowed chaff shall be driven away by the wind;
for the Lord guards the way of the just
but the way of the wicked leads to doom. ℟

Gospel Acclamation   Jn 8:31-32
Glory to you, O Christ, you are the Word of God.
If you make my word your home
you will indeed be my disciples,
and you will learn the truth, says the Lord.
Glory to you, O Christ, you are the Word of God.

Gospel

A reading from the holy Gospel according to Matthew 5:13-16
You are the light of the world.

Jesus said to his disciples: 'You are the salt of the earth. But if salt becomes tasteless, what can make it salty again? It is good for nothing, and can only be thrown out to be trampled underfoot by men.

'You are the light of the world. A city built on a hill-top cannot be hidden. No one lights a lamp to put it under a tub; they put it on the lamp-stand where it shines for everyone in the house. In the same way your light must shine in the sight of men, so that, seeing your good works, they may give the praise to your Father in heaven.'

This is the Gospel of the Lord.

Prayer over the Gifts
Lord, accept the gifts we bring on the feast of Saint David.
We offer them to win your forgiveness
and to give honour to your name.

PREFACE OF HOLY MEN AND WOMEN I

Father, all-powerful and ever-living God, we do well always and everywhere to give you thanks.

You are glorified in your saints, for their glory is the crowning of your gifts.
In their lives on earth you give us an example.
In our communion with them you give us their friendship.
In their prayer for the Church you give us strength and protection.
The great company of witnesses spurs us on to victory, to share their prize of everlasting glory, through Jesus Christ our Lord.

With angels and archangels and the whole company of saints we sing our unending hymn of praise:

Communion Antiphon   Mk 10:45
The Son of Man came to give his life as a ransom for all.

Proper of Saints: March

or   cf. Mt 19:27, 29

I assure you who left all and followed me; you will receive a hundredfold in return and inherit eternal life.

Prayer after Communion
All-powerful God,
you have strengthened us with this sacrament.
May we learn from Saint David's example
to seek you above all things,
and to live always as new men in Christ,
who lives and reigns for ever and ever.

Solemn Blessing or Prayer over the People (p.20)

4 March

St Casimir

Opening Prayer
All-powerful God,
to serve you is to reign:
by the prayers of Saint Casimir,
help us to serve you in holiness and justice.

Grant this through our Lord Jesus Christ, your Son,
who lives and reigns with you and the Holy Spirit,
one God, for ever and ever.

7 March

Ss Perpetua and Felicity, martyrs

Opening Prayer
Father,
your love gave the saints Perpetua and Felicity
courage to suffer a cruel martyrdom.
By their prayers, help us to grow in love of you.

We ask this through our Lord Jesus Christ, your Son,
who lives and reigns with you and the Holy Spirit,
one God, for ever and ever.

8 March

St John of God, religious

Opening Prayer
Father,
you gave John of God
love and compassion for others.
Grant that by doing good for others
we may be counted among the saints in your kingdom.

We ask this through out Lord Jesus Christ, your Son,
who lives and reigns with you and the Holy Spirit,
one God, for ever and ever.

9 March
St Frances of Rome, religious

Opening Prayer
Merciful Father,
in Frances of Rome
you have given us a unique
    example of love in marriage
as well as in religious life.
Keep us faithful in your service,
and help us to see and follow
    you
in all the aspects of life.

We ask this through out Lord
    Jesus Christ, your Son,
who lives and reigns with you
    and the Holy Spirit,
one God, for ever and ever.

10 March
Blessed John Ogilvie, Priest and Martyr

Opening Prayer
Almighty and eternal God,
you gave to blessed John wisdom
in defending the Catholic faith and
courage in facing a martyr's death:
listen to our prayers, and send us
an ever greater harvest of faith,
hope and love.

We ask this through our Lord Jesus
Christ, your Son, who lives and
reigns with you and the Holy Spirit,
one God, for ever and ever.

17 March
St Patrick, bishop, Patron of Ireland

Patrick, an apostle, making new beginnings of the Church in Ireland; Patrick, a bishop, consolidating what has been begun; Patrick, lover of the Irish people, creating a community of love and peace: such is the model before us today. His example and teaching is based on the scriptures and fidelity to the Church; the scriptures presenting the living face of Christ, the Church showing forth the presence of the risen Lord. 'Come, holy youth, and walk once more among us!'

Entrance Antiphon   Gen 12:1
Go from your country and your kindred and your father's house to the land that I will show you; and I will make you the father of a great people.

Opening Prayer
either
Let us pray
    (that like St Patrick the
    missionary, we will be
    fearless witnesses to the
    gospel of Jesus Christ)
God our Father,
you sent Saint Patrick to preach your glory to the people of Ireland. By the help of his prayers, may all Christians proclaim your love to all men.

Grant this through our Lord Jesus Christ, your Son, who lives and reigns with you and the Holy Spirit, one God, for ever and ever.

or

Let us pray
   (that, like Saint Patrick, we may be loyal to our faith in Christ)
Father in heaven,
you sent the great bishop Patrick to the people of Ireland to share his faith and to spend his life in loving service.

May our lives bear witness to the faith we profess, and our love bring others to the peace and joy of your gospel.

We ask this through Christ our Lord.

Liturgy of the Word
First Reading

A reading from the prophet Jeremiah 1:4-9
Go now to those to whom I send you.

The word of the Lord was addressed to me, saying,
'Before I formed you in the womb I knew you; before you came to birth I consecrated you; I have appointed you as prophet to the nations.'
I said, 'Ah, Lord God; look, I do not know how to speak: I am a child!'
But the Lord replied:
'Do not say, "I am a child."
Go now to those to whom I send you
and say whatever I command you.
Do not be afraid of them,
for I am with you to protect you—
it is the Lord who speaks!'

Then the Lord put out his hand and touched my mouth and said to me:
'There! I am putting my words into your mouth.'

This is the word of the Lord.

Responsorial Psalm Ps 116.
℟ *Mk 16:15*
℟ **Go out to all the world, and tell the Good News.**

or

Alleluia!

1. Alleluia!
   O praise the Lord, all you nations,
   acclaim him all you peoples! ℟

2. Strong is his love for us;
   he is faithful for ever. ℟

Second Reading

A reading from the Acts of the Apostles 13:46-49
We must turn to the pagans.

Paul and Barnabas spoke out boldly to the Jews. 'We had to proclaim the word of God to you first, but since you have rejected it, since you do not think yourselves worthy of eternal life, we must turn to the pagans. For this is what the Lord commanded us to do when he said:

'I have made you a light for the nations, so that my salvation may reach the ends of the earth.'

It made the pagans very happy to hear this and they thanked the Lord for his message; all who were destined for eternal life became believers. Thus the word of the Lord spread through the whole countryside.

This is the word of the Lord.

Gospel Acclamation   Lk 4:18-19
Alleluia, alleluia!
The Lord sent me to bring Good News to the poor, and freedom to prisoners.
Alleluia!

Gospel

A reading from the holy Gospel according to Luke   10:1-2.17-20
Your peace will rest on that man.

The Lord appointed seventy-two others and sent them out ahead of him, in pairs, to all the towns and places he himself was to visit. He said to them, 'The harvest is rich but the labourers are few, so ask the Lord of the harvest to send labourers to his harvest. Start off now, but remember, I am sending you out like lambs among wolves. Carry no purse, no haversack, no sandals. Salute no one on the road. Whatever house you go into, let your first words be, "Peace to this house!" And if a man of peace lives there, your peace will go and rest on him; if not, it will come back to you. Stay in the same house, taking what food and drink they have to offer, for the labourer deserves his wages; do not move from house to house. Whenever you go into a town where they make you welcome, eat what is set before you. Cure those in it who are sick, and say, "The kingdom of God is very near to you." But whenever you enter a town and they do not make you welcome, go out into the streets and say, "We wipe off the very dust of your town that clings to our feet, and leave it with you. Yet be sure of this: the kingdom of God is very near." I tell you, on that day it will not go as hard with Sodom as with that town.'

The seventy-two came back rejoicing. 'Lord,' they said 'even the devils submit to us when we use your name.' He said to them, 'I watched Satan fall like lightning from heaven. Yes, I have given you power to tread underfoot serpents and scorpions and the whole strength of the enemy; nothing shall ever hurt you. Yet do not rejoice that the spirits submit to you; rejoice rather that your names are written in heaven.'

This is the Gospel of the Lord.

The Profession of Faith is said.

Prayer over the Gifts
Lord our God,
by the power of this sacrament
deepen our love
and strengthen our faith:
as we celebrate the feast of Saint Patrick
bind us more and more to each other
in unity and peace.
Through Christ our Lord.

Amen.

PREFACE OF HOLY MEN AND WOMEN I

Father, all-powerful and ever-living God, we do well always and everywhere to give you thanks.

You are glorified in your saints, for their glory is the crowning of your gifts.

In their lives on earth you give us an example.

In our communion with them you give us their friendship.

In their prayer for the Church you give us strength and protection.

The great company of witnesses spurs us on to victory, to share their prize of everlasting glory, through Jesus Christ our Lord.

With angels and archangels and the whole company of saints we sing our unending hymn of praise.

Communion Antiphon
Cf. Lk 10:1.9
The Lord sent disciples to proclaim to the people: The Kingdom of God is very near to you.

Prayer after Communion
Lord,
by the power of this sacrament
strengthen our faith:
may all we do or say
proclaim your truth
in imitation of Saint Patrick,
who did not spare himself
but gave his whole life
to the preaching of your Word.
Through Christ our Lord.

Solemn Blessing or Prayer over the People (p.20)

18 March

St Cyril of Jerusalem, bishop and doctor of the Church

Opening Prayer
Father,
through Cyril of Jerusalem
you led your Church to a deeper understanding
of the mysteries of salvation.
Let his prayers help us to know your Son better
and to have eternal life in all its fullness.

We ask this through our Lord Jesus Christ, your Son,

who lives and reigns with you
  and the Holy Spirit,
one God, for ever and ever.

19 March

St Joseph, Husband of the Blessed Virgin Mary

Entrance Antiphon: Luke 12:42
The Lord has put his faithful servant in charge of his household.

Opening Prayer
Let us pray
that the Church will continue the saving work of Christ.

Father,
you entrusted our Saviour to the care of Saint Joseph.
By the help of his prayers
may your Church continue to serve its Lord, Jesus Christ,
who lives and reigns with you
  and the Holy Spirit,
one God, for ever and ever.

Liturgy of the Word

First Reading
A reading from the Book of Samuel.
            2 Sam 7:4-5.12-14.16
The Lord God will give him the throne of his ancestor David.

The word of the Lord came to Nathan:

'Go and tell my servant David, "Thus the Lord speaks: When your days are ended and you are laid to rest with your ancestors, I will preserve the offspring of your body after you and make his sovereignty secure. (It is he who shall build a house for my name, and I will make his royal throne secure for ever.) I will be a father to him and he a son to me. Your House and your sovereignty will always stand secure before me and your throne be established for ever."'

This the word of the Lord.

Responsorial Psalm
                    Ps 88:2-5.27.29
℟ **His dynasty shall last for ever.**

1 I will sing for ever of your love, O Lord;
   through all ages my mouth will proclaim your truth.
   Of this I am sure, that your love lasts for ever,
   that your truth is firmly established as the heavens. ℟

2 'I have made a covenant with my chosen one;
   I have sworn to David my servant:
   I will establish your dynasty for ever
   and set up your throne through all ages.' ℟

3 He will say to me: 'You are my father,
   my God, the rock who saves me.'
   I will keep my love for him always;

for him my covenant shall endure. ℟

Second Reading
A reading from the letter of St Paul to the Romans.
4:13.16-18.22
Though it seemed Abraham's hope could not be fulfilled, he hoped and he believed.

The promise of inheriting the world was not made to Abraham and his descendants on account of any law but on account of the righteousness which consists in faith. That is why what fulfils the promise depends on faith, so that it may be a free gift and be available to all of Abraham's descendants, not only those who belong to the Law but also those who belong to the faith of Abraham who is the Father of all of us. As scripture says: I have made you the ancestor of many nations — Abraham is our father in the eyes of God, in whom he put his faith, and who brings the dead to life and calls into being what does not exist.

Though it seemed Abraham's hope could not be fulfilled, he hoped and he believed, and through doing so he did become the father of many nations exactly as he had been promised: Your descendants will be as many as the stars. This is the faith that was 'considered as justifying him'.

This is the word of the Lord.

Gospel Acclamation   *Ps 83:5*
Glory and praise to you, O Christ!
They are happy who dwell in your house, O Lord, for ever singing your praise.
Glory and praise to you, O Christ!

Gospel

First Alternative
A reading from the holy Gospel according to St Matthew.
1:16.18-21.24
Joseph did what the angel of the Lord has told him to do.

Jacob was the father of Joseph the husband of Mary; of her was born Jesus who is called Christ.

This is how Jesus Christ came to be born. His mother Mary was betrothed to Joseph; but before they came to live together she was found to be with child through the Holy Spirit. Her husband Joseph, being a man of honour and wanting to spare her publicity, decided to divorce her informally. He had made up his mind to do this when the angel of Lord appeared to him in a dream and said, 'Joseph son of David, do not be afraid to take Mary home as your wife, because she has conceived what is in her by the Holy Spirit. She will give birth to a son and you must name him Jesus, because he is the one who is to save his people from their sins.' When Joseph woke up he did what the angel of the Lord had told him to do.

This is the Gospel of the Lord.

Second Alternative
A reading from the holy Gospel according to St Luke.
2:41-51
See how worried your father and I have been, looking for you.

Every year the parents of Jesus used to go to Jerusalem for the feast of the Passover. When he was twelve years old, they went up for the feast as usual. When they were on their way home after the feast, the boy Jesus stayed behind in Jerusalem without his parents knowing it. They assumed he was with the caravan, and it was only after a day's journey that they went to look for him among their relations and acquaintances. When they failed to find him they went back to Jerusalem looking for him everywhere.

Three days later, they found him in the Temple, sitting among the doctors, listening to them, and asking them questions; and all those who heard him were astounded at his intelligence and his replies. They were overcome when they saw him, and his mother said to him, 'My child, why have you done this to us? See how worried your father and I have been, looking for you.' 'Why were you looking for me?' he replied, 'Did you not know that I must be busy with my Father's affairs?' But they did not understand what he meant.

He then went down with them and came to Nazareth and lived under their authority.

This is the Gospel of the Lord.

Prayer over the Gifts
Father,
with unselfish love Saint Joseph
   cared for your Son,
born of the Virgin Mary.
May we also serve you at your
   altar with pure hearts.

PREFACE OF ST JOSEPH, HUSBAND OF MARY

Father, all-powerful and ever-
   living God,
we do well always and
   everywhere to give you
   thanks
as we honour Saint Joseph.

He is that just man,
that wise and loyal servant,
whom you placed at the head
   of your family.
With a husband's love he
   cherished Mary,
the virgin Mother of God.
With fatherly care he watched
   over Jesus Christ your Son,
conceived by the power of the
   Holy Spirit.

Through Christ the choirs of
   angels
and all the powers of heaven
praise and worship your glory.
May our voices blend with
   theirs

as we join in their unending hymn.

Communion Antiphon Mt 25:21
Come, good and faithful servant! Share the joy of your Lord!

Prayer after Communion
Lord,
today, you nourish us at this altar
as we celebrate the feast of Saint Joseph.
Protect your Church always,
and in your love watch over the gifts you have given us.

Solemn Blessing or Prayer over the People (p.20)

23 March
St Turibius of Mongrovejo, bishop

Opening Prayer
Lord,
through the apostolic work of Saint Turibius
and his unwavering love of truth,
you helped your Church to grow.
May your chosen people continue to grow
in faith and holiness.

Grant this through our Lord Jesus Christ, your Son,
who lives and reigns with you
    and the Holy Spirit,
one God, for ever and ever.

25 March
The Annunciation of the Lord

Entrance Antiphon
                    Hebrews 10:5-7
As Christ came into the world, he said: Behold! I have come to do your will, O God.

Opening Prayer
Let us pray
    (that we may become more like Christ
    who chose to become one of us)

Almighty Father of Our Lord Jesus Christ,
you have revealed the beauty of your power
by exalting the lowly virgin of Nazareth
and making her the mother of our Saviour.
May the prayers of this woman
bring Jesus to the waiting world
an fill the void of incompletion
with the presence of her child,
who lives and reigns with you
    and the Holy Spirit,
one God, for ever and ever.

Liturgy of the Word
First Reading   Isaiah 7:10-14
The maiden is with child.

The Lord spoke to Ahaz and said, 'Ask the Lord your God for a sign for yourself coming either from the depths of Sheol or from the heights above.' 'No,' Ahaz answered 'I will not put the Lord to the test.'

Then Isaiah said:

Listen now, House of David:
are you not satisfied with
   trying the patience of men
without trying the patience of
   my God, too?
The Lord himself, therefore,
will give you a sign.
It is this: the maiden is with
   child
and will soon give birth to a
   son
whom she will call
   Immanuel,
a name which means 'God-
is-with-us'.

This is the word of the Lord.

Responsional Psalm   Ps 39:7-11

℞ **Here I am, Lord,
I come to do your will.**

1 You do not ask for sacrifice
      and offerings,
   but an open ear.
   You do not ask for holocaust
      and victim.
   Instead, here am I. ℞

2 In the scroll of the book it
      stands written
   that I should do your will.
   My God, I delight in your
      law
   in the depth of my heart. ℞

3 Your justice I have
      proclaimed
   in the great assembly.
   My lips I have not sealed;
   you know it, O Lord. ℞

4 I have not hidden your
      justice in my heart
   but declared your faithful
      help.
   I have not hidden your love
      and your truth
   from the great assembly. ℞

Prayer after Communion
Lord,
may the sacrament we share
strengthen our faith and hope in
   Jesus, born of a virgin
and truly God and man.
By the power of his resurrection
may we come to eternal joy.

Second Reading
A reading from St Paul's letter
   to the Hebrews.   10:4-10
*I was commanded in the scroll
of the book, God, here I am!
   I am coming to obey your
will.'*

Bulls' blood and goats' blood are useless for taking away sin, and this is what Christ said, on coming into the world:

You who wanted no sacrifice
   or oblation,
prepared a body for me.
You took no pleasure in
   holocausts or sacrifices for
   sin;
then I said,
just as I was commanded in

the scroll of the book,
'God, here I am! I am
  coming to obey your will.'
Notice that he says first: You did not want what the Law lays down as the things to be offered, that is: the sacrifices, the oblations, the holocausts and the sacrifices for sin, and you took no pleasure in them; and then he says: Here I am! I am coming to obey your will. He is abolishing the first sort to replace it with the second. And this will was for us to be made holy by the offering of his body made once and for all by Jesus Christ.

This is the word of the Lord.

Gospel Acclamation
Praise to you, O Christ, king of
  eternal glory!
The Word was made flesh,
he lived among us,
and we saw his glory.
Praise to you, O Christ, king of
  eternal glory!

Gospel
A reading from the holy Gospel according to St Luke

Listen! You are to conceive and bear a son   Lk 1:26-38

The angel Gabriel was sent by God to a town in Galilee called Nazareth, to a virgin betrothed to a man named Joseph of the House of David; and the virgin's name was Mary. He went in and said to her, 'Rejoice, so highly favoured! The Lord is with you.' She was deeply disturbed by these words and asked herself what this greeting could mean, but the angel said to her, 'Mary, do not be afraid; you have won God's favour. Listen! You are to conceive and bear a son, and you must name him Jesus. He will be great and will be called Son of the Most High. The Lord God will give him the throne of his ancestor David; he will rule over the House of Jacob for ever and his reign will have no end.' Mary said to the angel, 'But how can this come about, since I am a virgin?' 'The Holy Spirit will come upon you' the angel answered 'and the power of the Most High will cover you with its shadow. And so the child will be holy and will be called Son of God. Know this too: your kinswoman Elizabeth has, in her old age, herself conceived a son, and she whom people called barren is now in her sixth month, for nothing is impossible to God.' 'I am the handmaid of the Lord,' said Mary 'let what you have said be done to me.' And the angel left her.

This is the Gospel of the Lord.

In the profession of faith, all genuflect at the words, 'and was made man'.

Prayer over the Gifts
Almighty Father,
as we recall the beginning of
  the Church
when your Son became man,
may we celebrate with joy
  today
this sacrament of your love.

PREFACE OF THE ANNUNCIATION

Father, all-powerful and ever-living God,
we do well always and everywhere to give you thanks
through Jesus Christ our Lord.

He came to save mankind by becoming a man himself.
The Virgin Mary, receiving the angel's message in faith,
conceived by the power of the Spirit
and bore your Son in purest love.
In Christ, the eternal truth, your promise to Israel came true.
In Christ, the hope of all peoples,
man's hope was realised beyond all expectation.

Through Christ the angels of heaven
offer their prayer of adoration
as they rejoice in your presence for ever.
May our voices be one with theirs
in their triumphant hymn of praise.

Communion Antiphon
                      Isaiah 7:14
The Virgin is with child and shall bear a son, and she will call him Emmanuel.

Prayer after Communion
Father,
in this eucharist we touch the divine life you give to the world.
Help us to follow Christ with love to eternal life where he is Lord for ever and ever.

Solemn Blessing or Prayer over the People (p.20)

APRIL

2 April

St Francis of Paola, hermit

Opening Prayer
Father of the lowly,
you raised Saint Francis of Paola to the glory of your saints.
By his example and prayers,
may we come to the rewards you have promised the humble.

We ask this through our Lord Jesus Christ, your Son,
who lives and reigns with you and the Holy Spirit,
one God, for ever and ever.

4 April

St Isidore, bishop and doctor of the Church

Opening Prayer
Lord,
hear the prayers we offer in commemoration of Saint Isidore.
May your Church learn from his teaching

and benefit from his intercession.

Grant this through our Lord Jesus Christ, your Son,
who lives and reigns with you and the Holy Spirit,
one God, for ever and ever.

5 April

St Vincent Ferrer, priest

Opening Prayer
Father,
you called Saint Vincent Ferrer
to preach the gospel of the last judgment.
Through his prayers may we come with joy
to meet your Son in the kingdom of heaven,
where he lives and reigns with you and the Holy Spirit,
one God, for ever and ever.

7 April

St John Baptist de la Salle, priest
Memorial

Opening Prayer
Father,
you chose Saint John Baptist de la Salle
to give young people a Christian education.
Give your Church teachers who will devote themselves
to helping your children grow as Christian men and women.

We ask this through our Lord Jesus Christ, your Son,
who lives and reigns with you and the Holy Spirit,
one God, for ever and ever.

11 April

St Stanislaus, bishop and martyr

Opening Prayer
Father,
to honour you, Saint Stanislaus faced martyrdom with courage.
Keep us strong and loyal in our faith until death.

Grant this through our Lord Jesus Christ, your Son,
who lives and reigns with you and the Holy Spirit,
one God, for ever and ever.

13 April

St Martin I, pope and martyr

Opening Prayer
Merciful God, our Father,
neither hardship, pain, nor the threat of death
could weaken the faith of Saint Martin.
Through our faith, give us courage
to endure whatever sufferings the world may inflict upon us.

We ask this through our Lord Jesus Christ, your Son,
who lives and reigns with you and the Holy Spirit,
one God, for ever and ever.

A CELEBRATION OF THE SACRAMENT OF PENANCE DURING LENT

BE CONVERTED AND LIVE

INTRODUCTORY RITES

Song
When the faithful have assembled, they may sing a psalm, antiphon or other appropriate song while the priest is entering the church.

Sign of the Cross
In the name of the Father, and of the Son, and of the Holy Spirit, Amen.

Greeting:
Grace and peace be with you
from God our Father
and from the Lord Jesus Christ
who laid down his life for our sins.

And also with you.

Admonition
Then the priest or another minister speaks briefly about the importance and purpose of the celebration and the order of the service.

Opening Prayer
The priest invites all to pray, using these or similar words:
Brothers and sisters, God calls us to conversion; let us therefore ask him for the grace of sincere repentance.

All pray in silence for a brief period. Then the priest sings or says the prayer:

Father of mercies
and God of all consolation,
you do not wish the sinner to die
  but to be converted and live.
Come to the aid of your people,
  that they may turn from their
  sins and live for you alone.
May we be attentive to your word,
  confess our sins, receive your
  forgiveness, and be always
  grateful for your loving
  kindness.
Help us to live the truth in love and
  grow into the fullness of Christ,
  your Son, who lives and reigns
  for ever and ever. **Amen.**

LITURGY OF THE WORD

First Reading
A reading from the book of Deuteronomy.   30:15-20
I set before you life and prosperity, death and disaster.
'See today I set before you life and prosperity, death and disaster. If you obey the commandments of the Lord your God that I enjoin on you today, if you love the Lord your God and follow his ways, if you keep his commandments, his laws, his customs, you will live and increase, and the Lord your God will bless you in the land which you are entering to make your own. But if your heart strays, if you refuse to listen, if you let yourself be drawn into worshipping other gods and serving them, I tell you today, you will

most certainly perish; you will not live long in the land you are crossing the Jordan to enter and possess. I call heaven and earth to witness against you today: I set before you life or death, blessing or curse. Choose life, then, so that you and your descendants may live, in the love of the Lord your God, obeying his voice, clinging to him; for in this your life consists, and on this depends your long stay in the land which the Lord swore to your fathers Abraham, Isaac and Jacob he would give them.'

This is the word of the Lord.
C **Thanks be to God.**

Responsorial Psalm *Ps 129:* ℟ *v.17*
℟ **With the Lord there is mercy, and fullness of redemption.**

1 Out of the depths I cry to you,
   O Lord, Lord, hear my voice!
   O let your ears be attentive
   to the voice of my pleading. ℟

2 If you, O Lord, should mark our guilt,
   Lord, who would survive?
   But with you is found forgiveness:
   for this we revere you. ℟

3 My soul is waiting for the Lord,
   I count on his word.
   My soul is longing for the Lord
   more than watchman for daybreak. ℟

4 Because with the Lord there is mercy and fullness of redemption,
   Israel indeed he will redeem from all its iniquity. ℟

Second Reading
A reading from the letter to the Hebrews. *3:12-19.4:1-3*
God's place of rest for his faithful people.

Take care, brothers, that there is not in any one of your community a wicked mind, so unbelieving as to turn away from the living God. Every day, as long as this 'today' lasts, keep encouraging one another so that none of you is hardened by the lure of sin, because we shall remain co-heirs with Christ only if we keep a grasp on our first confidence right to the end.

This is the word of the Lord.
C **Thanks be to God.**

Gospel Acclamation *Jn 8:12*

I am the light of the world.
Anyone who follows me will have the light of life.

Gospel *Lk 5:27-32*
A reading from the holy Gospel according to Luke

I have not come to call the virtuous, but sinners to repentance.

When Jesus went out after this, he noticed a tax collector, Levi by name, sitting by the customs house, and said to him, 'Follow me'. And leaving everything he got up and followed him. In his honour Levi held a great reception in his house, and with them at table was a large gathering of tax collectors and others. The Pharisees and their scribes complained to his disciples and said, 'Why do you eat and drink with tax collectors and sinners?' Jesus said to them in reply, 'It is not those who are well who need the doctor, but the sick. I have not come

to call the virtuous, but sinners to repentance.
This is the Gospel of the Lord.
Praise to you, Lord Jesus Christ.

Homily

Examination of Conscience
The following examination of conscience in the form of a Litany may be used:

The Lord says:
'You shall love the Lord your God with your whole heart'.
When I fail to set my heart on God, and do not love him above all things, and I am unfaithful to his commandments: Lord, have mercy.
Lord, have mercy.

When I forget that God has spoken through his son; when my faith in God and in the Church's teaching is insecure: Lord, have mercy.
Lord, have mercy.

When my love and respect for God's holy name is wanting, and I fail to observe his Day in the way he wishes: Lord, have mercy.
Lord, have mercy.

Christ says:
'Love one another as I have loved you'.
When I lack genuine love for family, parents, husband, wife, children, and the needy: Christ, have mercy.
Christ, have mercy.

When my life does not reflect the mission I received in confirmation, so that I do not spread the gospel, or promote the good of the community in which I live, nor give of my best to my work and profession: Christ, have mercy.
Christ, have mercy.

When my attitudes to authority, responsibility, truth, justice, property, and the reputation of others are defective or wanting: Christ, have mercy.
Christ, have mercy.

Christ our Lord says:
'Be perfect as your Father is perfect'.
When my life's direction is uncertain, and I do not grow in the life of the Spirit, in prayer, in the grace of the sacraments; when I pay only lip-service to God's word and do not devote myself to good works and self-denial. Lord, have mercy.
Lord, have mercy.

When I misuse time, health, strength and talents; when I am impatient with life's sufferings and disappointments: Lord, have mercy.
Lord, have mercy.

When I do not keep senses and body pure and chaste as a temple of God's Spirit; when my conscience is not formed by God's word and the Church's teaching; when I do not enjoy true freedom

by obeying God's law and following the promptings of the Spirit, but instead I am a slave to the evil within me: Lord, have mercy.
Lord, have mercy.

Liturgy of Reconciliation

General Confession of Sins
My brothers and sisters, confess your sins and pray for each other, that you may be healed.
I confess to almighty God,
and to you, my brothers and sisters,
that I have sinned through my own fault
They strike their breast:
in my thoughts and in my words,
in what I have done,
and in what I have failed to do;
and I ask blessed Mary, ever virgin,
all the angels and saints,
and you, my brothers and sisters,
to pray for me to the Lord our God.

Deacon or minister:
Brothers and sisters, let us call to mind the goodness of God our Father, and acknowledge our sins, so that we may receive his merciful forgiveness.

I confess . . .
God who is infinitely merciful pardons all who are repentant and takes away their guilt. We are confident in his goodness.

Let us confess our sins with sincerity of heart:
Lord, hear our prayer.
Lord, hear our prayer.
Give us the grace of true repentance.
Lord, hear our prayer.
Pardon your servants and release them from the debt of sin.
Lord, hear our prayer.
Forgive your children who confess their sins, and restore them to full communion with your Church.
Lord, hear our prayer.
Renew the glory of baptism in those who have lost it by sin.
Lord, hear our prayer.
Welcome them to your altar, and renew their spirit with the hope of eternal glory.
Lord, hear our prayer.
Keep them faithful to your sacraments and loyal in your service.
Lord, hear our prayer.
Renew your love in their hearts, and make them bear witness to it in their daily lives.
Lord, hear our prayer.
Keep them always obedient to your commandments and protect within them your gift of eternal life.
Lord, hear our prayer.

Let us now pray to God our Father in the words Christ gave us, and ask him for his forgiveness and protection from all evil.

Our Father . . .
The Priest concludes:
Father, our source of life,
you know our weakness.

May we reach out with joy to grasp your hand and walk more readily in your ways.
We ask this through Christ our Lord.
Amen.

Individual Confession and Absolution
God, the Father of mercies,
through the death and resurrection of his Son has reconciled the world to himself and sent the Holy Spirit among us for the forgiveness of sins;
through the ministry of the Church may God give you pardon and peace,
and I absolve you from your sins in the name of the Father, and of the Son, and of the Holy Spirit.
Amen.

When the individual confessions have been completed, it is fitting for all to sing a psalm or hymn or to say a litany in acknowledgement of God's power and mercy.

Concluding Prayer of Thanksgiving

Almighty and merciful God,
how wonderfully you created man
and still more wonderfully remade him.
You do not abandon the sinner
but seek him out with a father's love.
You sent your Son into the world
to destroy sin and death
by his passion,
and to restore life and joy
by his resurrection.
You sent the Holy Spirit into our hearts
to make us your children
and heirs of your kingdom.
You constantly renew our spirit
in the sacraments of your redeeming love,
freeing us from slavery to sin
and transforming us ever more closely
into the likeness of your beloved Son.
We thank you for the wonders of your mercy,
and with heart and hand and voice
we join with the whole Church
in a new song of praise:
Glory to you
through Christ
in the Holy Spirit,
now and for ever.
Amen.

CONCLUDING RITE

The Blessing
Then the priest blesses all present:
and may the blessing of almighty God,
the Father, and the Son, ✠
and the Holy Spirit,
come upon you and remain with you
for ever.
Amen.

The Dismissal

Go in peace to love and serve the Lord.
Thanks be to God.

STATIONS OF THE CROSS

Pope John Paul II

We retrace Jesus' journey along the *via dolorosa* from Pilate's palace to the hill of Golgotha.

He went along this way as a man condemned to death on the cross, bent beneath the weight of the ignominious instrument of his own execution. He was accompanied by a group of soldiers who were to be his executioners. On this sorrowful way, his enemies, those who had brought about his death, could afford to remain in the background. They had all the advantages over Jesus' friends who could do little to console him or relieve him of his burden.

> As the crowds were appalled on seeing him
> — so disfigured did he look
> that he seemed no longer human —
>
> Is 52:14

Only once did this sad procession wind its way through the narrow streets of Jerusalem. Once and only once was Jesus of Nazareth crucified. But the way of the cross continues and all over the world, new processions daily wend their way along it. We are, here and now, just one such procession.

And while Jesus sits in glory at the right hand of the Father and the cross no longer stands on the hill of Golgotha, the mystery of Christ's death on that cross is constantly being fulfilled. Through this mystery redemption is offered to all human beings so that in him each one of us may discover our way: in the midsts of the trials of our earthly existence we may find the way to our eternal destiny.

Let us pray

All powerful and eternal God, who gave as a model to humanity Christ your Son and our saviour, become man and humiliated even unto death on the cross, grant that through the trials of life we may share more intimately in his redemptive passion and thus reach the glory of his resurrection.

Through Christ our Lord, Amen.

FIRST STATION

Jesus is condemned to death by Pilate

P We adore thee, O Christ, and bless thee.

C Because through your holy cross you have redeemed the world.

Pontius Pilate — the Roman Governor — hesitates before pronouncing the death sentence on Jesus of Nazareth. He is not convinced of the charges levelled against Jesus by his accusers. He condemns him to be flogged, hoping to release him later. Flogged, and crowned with thorns, Pilate shows Jesus to the crowd again.

His words are on record: *'Ecce Homo*, Behold the man,' (cf. Jn 19:5). The people's insistent cry becomes more strident: 'Crucify him! crucify him!' Pilate gives in.

He was unaware that when John the Baptist saw Jesus on the banks of the river Jordan he had proclaimed to the people: 'Look, there is the lamb of God that takes away the sins of the world' (Jn 1:29). But the human injustice represented by Pilate's decision finds a new context in the mystery of the sacrifice of the Lamb of God.

Eternal love works through our injustice. 'God loved the world so much that he gave his only Son. . .' (Jn 3:16), to be condemned by Pilate to death on the cross for the redemption of the world.

Let us pray,
Lamb of God, who takes away the sins of the world, grant that we may not condemn you anew to death through our sins. Grant that through your death we may have life!

All: Our Father. . .

> At the cross her station keeping,
> Stood the mournful Mother weeping,
> Close to Jesus to the last.

SECOND STATION

The cross is laid on the shoulders of Jesus

P We adore thee, O Christ, and bless thee.

C Because through your holy cross you have redeemed the world.

The sins of the world are wiped out through the cross. And now the executioners prepare for their task. They remove the red mantle from Jesus' shoulders. The mantle had been part of Pilate's mockery. Jesus' own clothes are put back on him and the heavy cross is placed on his shoulders.

Weighed down by the cross he sets out through the streets of Jerusalem for the hill of Golgotha. Jesus of Nazareth: 'Like a sapling he grew in front of us, like a root in arid ground'. (Is 53:2)

The cross sprouts from this root. At the end of his earthly pilgrimage Jesus of Nazareth becomes one with the cross. He becomes one with the cross, synonymous with the cross as a unique sign of salvation for the world. The sins of the world are to be wiped out by the cross of the Lamb of God.

From the moment when Jesus accepts the cross, the mystery of the redemption of the world approaches its culmination, the high point of the history of humanity.

Let us go out into the streets of the city. Let us enter even deeper into this mystery.

Let us pray,
Sweet Lord, Jesus Christ, all patient Lamb of God, remind humanity once again of the truth of your cross!

All: Our Father. . .

> Through her heart, his sorrow sharing,
> All his bitter anguish bearing,
> Now at length the sword had passed.

THIRD STATION

Jesus falls for the first time

P We adore thee, O Christ, and bless thee.

C Because through your holy cross you have redeemed the world.

The significance of the cross is given full expression when Jesus falls on the way to Golgotha. The cross weighs down on us. Its weight is greater than our strength. We fall beneath the cross. Jesus falls under the weight of his cross. 'He was despised and rejected by men; a man of sorrows, and familiar with suffering, a man to make people screen their faces; he was despised and we took no account of him. (Is 53:3)

Shortly before this 'he gave orders' to the wind and to the waves' (Lk 8:25), exorcised the possessed, cured the sick, restored sight and hearing, raised the dead and called Lazarus forth from the tomb. He gave proof of divine power and 'taught them with authority'. (Mk 1:22)

But now another expression of power is needed for the redemption of the world through the cross: this is the power that shows itself through weakness (cf. 2 Cor 12:9). It is precisely this power which we see when Jesus falls beneath the cross.

And yet another sign is needed for the redemption of the world. It is the sign of silence:

> 'Harshly dealt with, he bore it humbly, never opened his mouth;
> like a lamb that is led to the slaughter-house,
> like a sheep that is dumb before its shearers
> never opening its mouth.' (Is 53:7)

Power through weakness and the sign of silence, this is the meaning of the first fall.

Let us pray,
Teach us continuously this truth: strength is forged in weakness. Teach us to get up again when we fall.

All: Our Father. . .

> Oh, how sad and sore distressed
> was that Mother highly blest
> Of the sole-begotten One!

FOURTH STATION

Jesus meets his mother

P We adore thee, O Christ, and bless thee.

C Because through your holy cross you have redeemed the world.

'Did you not know that I must be busy with my Father's affairs?' (Lk 2:49)

This was Jesus' answer to the reprimand from Mary and Joseph when he was lost in the Temple in Jerusalem. And now, behold Mary who 'stored up all these things in her heart' (Lk 2:51). Here is Mary of whom it was said 'Blessed is she who believed' (Lk 1:45); the same Mary in Nazareth, in Bethlehem, during the flight into Egypt and again back in Nazareth. Now she is on the *way of the cross*. Son, why have you done this to us. . .? the mother asked her twelve-year-old son. And now this cross, this sorrowful, ignominious procession to death on the cross. . . are these realities 'my father's business'? Was it to this he alluded as a twelve-year-old?

Mary does not ask. Mary believes. Indeed, he is about his father's business, Jesus, 'her own Son!' In all this Mary is with him.

Let us pray,
O Mary, you whose life was an act of faith, help us to find through our faith the answers to life's most difficult problems. Be with us now and forever.

All: Hail Mary. . .

> Christ above in torment hangs;
> She beneath beholds the pangs
> Of her dying glorious Son.

FIFTH STATION

Simon of Cyrene helps Jesus to carry his cross

P We adore thee, O Christ, and bless thee.

C Because through your holy cross you have redeemed the world.

'Anyone who does not take his cross and follow in my footsteps is not worthy of me' (Mt 10:38).

Simon of Cyrene does not wish to take up his cross with Jesus. He does not want to be considered 'worthy'. One's dignity is not enhanced by helping a condemned man to carry the very cross on which he will die. He is constrained by the soldiers. He is forced into carrying the cross. (cf Mt 27:32)

How readily each one of us may recognise ourselves in Simon! We flee from the cross. We shun even minimal exposure to suffering. We do not want to experience humiliation.

For Jesus of Nazareth the way of the cross was a necessary part of his proclamation of the Gospel of suffering. Simon, feel for this man of suffering! Help him! Throw off all outside constraints and replace them with an interior change of heart. Suffer with him ! Who knows, your soul may learn to see the truth. Perhaps, in due course you will become 'worthy' of him with whom you carry the cross.

Let us pray,
Jesus, teach us to carry your cross together with all those suffering human beings, who, through your will we meet on the road of life. Grant us real conversion of heart!

All: Our Father. . .

> Is there one who would not weep,
> Whelmed in miseries so deep
> Christ's dear Mother to behold?

SIXTH STATION

Veronica wipes the face of Jesus

P We adore thee, O Christ, and bless thee.

C Because through your holy cross you have redeemed the world.

Yet another example of those women about whom Jesus said: 'Why are you upsetting the woman? What she has done for me is one of the good works indeed!' *(Mt 26:10)*

The Gospels are silent about the good deed in question but tradition has linked it forever to the way of the cross. Veronica's name reminds us that on the veil with which she wiped the condemned man's face, a special image of that face remained. Jesus' sweat and blood imprinted the image of his face on the veil.

This image bears witness to a central Christian truth: on every act of love there is imprinted the face of Christ. This imprint remains in the human heart, on the human conscience. These acts of love are our Veronica's veil awaiting the sign of redemption. Our human conscience bears the seal of love. Christ the Redeemer is the spouse of all human souls. He awaits a loving response like that of Veronica on the way of the cross.

Let us pray,
O Jesus, teach us to love even when we are suffering. Teach us to love especially when we are suffering!

All: Our Father. . .

> Can the human heart refrain
> From partaking in her pain,
> In that Mother's pain untold?

SEVENTH STATION

Jesus falls for the second time

P We adore thee, O Christ, and bless thee.

C Because through your holy cross you have redeemed the world.

'And yet ours were the sufferings he bore, ours the sorrows he carried. But we, we thought of him as someone punished, struck by God and brought low. Yet he was pierced through for our faults, crushed for our sins' (Is 53:4ff).

What is the inner truth of the cross of Jesus? What is the significance of his falling on the way to Golgotha? It is the self-same truth that is proclaimed in that moving canticle of the 'suffering servant' in the Book of Isaiah. In our eyes condemned and therefore guilty. Human justice has appeared to win — but what of divine jutice?

The deepest emotion that the human heart can reach when faced with this suffering beneath the weight of the cross, when witnessing his falls, is *compassion*. It is possible to go beyond this only with the eyes of faith that penetrate the mystery. Thus the Prophet is able to explain: Behold the man who falls beneath his cross, this man atones for sins — but not for his own sins.

'But he was wounded for our transgressions, he was bruised for our iniquities'.

In this fall — and our falls are our sins — he unites himself with every member of the human race. Yet he is himself without sin. He falls in order to raise us up. He falls so that we are enabled to pick ourselves up. Every fall beneath the cross is given its full meaning in the context of the divine mystery of redemption.

Let us pray,

Let us not harden our hearts, O Lord. Let us see our falls, our sins, and our guilt in the light of your falls beneath the weight of the cross. Enlighten our conscience; give us the grace of conversion.

All: Our Father. . .

> Bruised, derided, cursed, defiled,
> She beheld her tender Child
> All with bloody scourges rent.

EIGHTH STATION

Jesus consoles the women of Jerusalem

P We adore thee, O Christ, and bless thee.

C Because through your holy cross you have redeemed the world.

Jesus says: Daughters of Jerusalem 'do not weep for me, weep rather for yourselves and for your children' (Lk 23:28).

These are strange words: words of consolation but with a strong element of warning. This warning becomes even more ominous 'for the days will surely come when people will say, "Happy are those who are barren, the wombs that have never borne, the breasts that have never suckled!" Then they will begin to say to the mountains, "Fall on us!" to the hills "Cover us!". For if men use the green wood like this, what will happen when it is dry?' (Lk 23:29-31)

Such is Jesus' reaction to the tearful lamentations of the women of Jerusalem as they accompany him on his sorrowful way.

With these words he envisages all the sorrows which will befall us on pilgrimage into a distant future. He is thinking as much of the future of the world as of the future of Jerusalem.

All our sufferings, coupled with the setbacks of our human world — the legacy of sin — come together in the sufferings of Jesus. He is the 'green wood'. In him a new reign of justice is revealed. In him is new life. From his cross redemption pours over us all.

Thus the words of warning to the women of Jerusalem — and they were serious in their import — are also bearers of a message of hope and brighter things. 'Do not weep', he says. These are words of consolation addressed to all those who are engaged in the fruitless struggles of existence. They are addressed to a threatened humanity.

Let us pray,
Jesus Christ, be with us through all times. Grant that the trials which life brings our way may be enlightened by the light of your Gospel.

All: Our Father. . .

> Let me share with thee his pain,
> Who for all my sins was slain,
> Who for me in torments died.

NINTH STATION

Jesus falls a third time

P We adore thee, O Christ, and bless thee.

C Because through your holy cross you have redeemed the world.

> We had all gone astray,
> each taking his own way,
> and Yahweh burdened him
> with the sins of all of us.
>
> (Is 53:6)

Jesus falls a third time on his sorrowful journey. Each time he falls he grows more weary. He falls beneath the weight of his cross but at the same time he falls beneath the weight of our sins: 'Truly the Lord has laid on him the iniquity of us all.'

Thus spoke Isaiah, the prophet of the Old Testament, almost as if he were an eyewitness, a fifth evangelist. Yet it was the will of the Lord to bruise him; he has put him to grief (Ibid v 10), the book of Isaiah continues. Could one have described Jesus' third fall beneath the cross with greater realism? And yet this realism comes face to face with a baffling mystery. 'For our sake God made the sinless one into sin, so that in him we might become the goodness of God (2 Cor 5:21).

This is why Jesus is crushed beneath his sufferings: Though he did not know sin, on his sorrowful way of the cross he experienced what terrible suffering sin represents. This he experienced. It was lived within the heart of this man-God.

Let us pray,

Jesus Christ, fallen for the third time beneath your cross, we ask you, on behalf of all human hearts, for the grace of contrition for our sins, for the grace of saving repentance.

All: Our Father. . .

> O thou Mother! fount of love!
> Touch my spirit from above,
> Make my heart with thine accord.

TENTH STATION

Jesus is stripped of his garments

P We adore thee, O Christ, and bless thee.

C Because through your holy cross you have redeemed the world.

'And when they had reached a place called Golgotha, that is, the place of the skull, they gave him wine to drink mixed with gall, which he tasted but refused to drink. When they had finished crucifying him they shared out his clothing by casting lots' (Mt 27:33-35).

Jesus declines the sense-dulling drink offered by his executioners. His desire is to experience, even on a human level, the fullness of his suffering. He does not wish to dilute, even in the smallest way, the full torture of crucifixion. The crucifixion was to embrace his entire body. It was to reach the depths of his existence, lead him to final prostration and annihilation. This is the body of which the Psalmist said,

> You who wanted no sacrifice or oblation,
> prepared a body for me.
> You took no pleasure in holocausts or sacrifices for sin;
> then I said,
> just as I was commanded in the scroll of the book,
> 'God, here I am! I am coming to obey your will.'
> *Heb 10:5-7; cf Ps 40:6-8*

On the hill of Golgotha this body has been stripped of all clothing. The wounds of the flagellation are open and raw. On his head is a crown of thorns. In this body is fulfilled the destiny of the Paschal lamb. This body is to be immolated as a sacrifice to the point of complete self-abnegation. This is the sacrifice of the new and eternal testament. The body is given for the sins of the world. The body through which 'the old man' is transformed and readied to become a new man.

The body which will remain with us as a sacrament, as food and as Eucharist.

Let us pray,

O Lord, through the merits of your martyred body grant that we may grasp the truth of the fact that our bodies are the temple of the Holy Spirit who lives in us (*cf 1 Cor 6:19ff*). Grant that we may live according to this truth!

All: Our Father...

> Make me feel as thou hast felt;
> Make my soul to glow and melt
> With the love of Christ my Lord.

ELEVENTH STATION

Jesus is nailed to the cross

P We adore thee, O Christ, and bless thee.

C Because through your holy cross you have redeemed the world.

> They tear holes in my hands and my feet...
> I can count every one of my bones
>
> *Ps 22:16-18*

When Jesus fell on the road to Golgotha the cross was a burden that weighed him to the ground. Now it is different. He is 'raised up' (*Jn 12:32*) on the cross. His body is fixed to its gallows. He can no longer move or bend or seek the doubtful solace of falling on the ground. This body is condemned to hours of suffering, suffering that goes on during this agony of the cold embrace in the rigid arms of the cross.

Let us remind ourselves of the words of the Psalmist and of the Prophet. We might also call to mind the most recent modern findings on the torture of the agony and crucifixion on Golgotha.

But the full reality of the passion remains outside the scope of any human examination. The full reality of that mystery — hidden before all time in God — is the mystery which on Golgotha reached the fullness of time.

'Amor meus — pondus meum' the words of the great St Augustine spring to mind. 'The love that is in me is what weighs me down.' (*Confessions XIII, 9, 2*). These words seem to reach the core of the mystery: the cross weighed on his Body; his body now weighs on the cross. In both cases it is a weight of love — *Amor pondus* — love weighs down! It is necessary therefore 'because nothing the world has to offer — the sensual body, the lustful eye, pride in possessions — could ever come from the Father' (*1 Jn 2:16*) once and for all to be counterbalanced by the weight of this love: love that is nailed to the cross as the Body of Christ. Through this mysterious weight nailed to the cross, the world is redeemed forever. And along our wayward paths and through our faltering steps this love leads towards our final destination in God. In God himself.

Let us pray,
Spirit of truth, grant that we may always feel the weight of Christ's saving cross. Grant that we may be enabled to penetrate the darkness of human history aided by the light of the crucified Christ.

All: Our Father. . .

> Holy Mother! pierce me through:
> In my heart each wound renew
> Of my Saviour crucified.

TWELFTH STATION

Jesus dies on the cross

P We adore thee, O Christ, and bless thee.

C Because through your holy cross you have redeemed the world.

'. . .he was humbler yet, even to accepting death, death on a cross'. (Phil 2:8)

He accepted death, he accepted real human death. He chose death, death on the cross. Paul the Apostle has this to say: 'His state was divine, yet he did not cling to his equality with God' (Phil 2:6).

He did not call on immortality. God is immortal. God is life.

And yet Jesus Christ — equal to God in his divinity as son of the Father became like us according to his humanity — he chose death. He accepted death, that same death which is the lot of every human being.

In dying he 'stripped himself' according to his own free choice. He accepted death, the lot of all humanity. He inserted death into his own history, just as death is part of everyone's own history. He accepted death as inherited from Adam. In this way he became completely and definitively 'as men are' (Phil 2:7).

In his human likeness, achieved through death, he was perfectly obedient! Obedience that brings salvation. Through this obedience 'unto death' he overcame death. He overcame death because he conquered sin. Sin has its root in our disobedience to the Father our Creator and its fruit is death.

Overcome by unimaginable suffering Jesus dies on the cross. His sufferings embrace his whole being and he cries out 'My God, My God, why have you deserted me?' (Mk 27:46; Mt 15:34). For this very reason his sufferings have saving power. They reach inwards and outwards and embrace all that has been enslaved by the destructive powers of sin, by the disobedience of the creature to the Father, his creator. This disobedience is cancelled out by his infinite act of obedience and filial love.

In this way the Son restores humanity and the world to the Father. So also he reconciles the Father to humanity and to the world. He accepts death as the human lot, as part of our inheritance, as intrinsic to our history. Through his death he again receives the gift of life from the Father: the beginning of the new earth and new heaven.

Jesus dies on the cross, he gives up the spirit. 'It is accomplished' (Jn 19:30). 'Father, into thy hands I commit my spirit' (Lk 23:36). This is the greatest hour in the history of the created universe.

Let us pray,
We proclaim your death, O Lord, Jesus Christ. Grant that we may live that life made possible for us by your death on the cross.

All: Our Father. . .

> For the sins of His own nation,
> Saw Him hang in desolation,
> Till His Spirit forth He sent.

THIRTEENTH STATION

Jesus is taken down from the cross and placed in the arms of his mother

P We adore thee, O Christ, and bless thee.

C Because through your holy cross you have redeemed the world.

Mary! Once again that body which the eternal Son assumed in your virginal womb is returned to your maternal embrace.

> 'You who wanted no sacrifice or oblation, prepared a body for me.'

You held him in your arms as an infant, newborn in Bethlehem. Even then, through Herod's agents, death threatened him. Now death has overtaken him before your very eyes, Holy Mother! And as a result of that death his body is now placed in your arms. Your own heart as a mother shared this death just as it shared in the birth of the Emmanuel. By force and by law he was taken; would anyone plead his cause? Yes, he was torn away from the land of the living; for our faults struck down in death.' (Is 53:8)

> You see this child: he is destined for the fall
> and for the rising of many in Israel,
> destined to be a sign that is rejected' (*Lk 2:34*)

We salute you, Mother, united with Christ in his passion and death, united with him in the work of our redemption and the saving of the world.

Let us pray,
O Mother, in your presence our thoughts and emotions become more clear and meaningful. May they be enlightened by the light of the cross of Christ as reflected from your immaculate heart.

All: Our Father. . .

> Let me mingle tears with thee,
> Mourning Him who mourned for me
> All the days that I may live.

FOURTEENTH STATION

Jesus is laid in the tomb

P We adore thee, O Christ, and bless thee.

C Because through your holy cross you have redeemed the world.

> For you will not leave my soul among the dead,
> nor let your beloved know decay. (*Ps 15:10*)

The body of Jesus, now removed from the cross, is wrapped in the burial shroud. Let us take part in the burial of this body, the action in which Jesus emptied himself, becoming obedient even unto death. His burial marks the ultimate phase of his act of obedience.

Just as he accepted human death, now he accepts the tomb offered to him by Joseph of Arimathea, a man of good will. Tombs shield from our view the gradual process of decomposition. The tomb of Jesus of Nazareth also serves for a while to shield from our view the mystery of faith: the descent into hell which we proclaim in the acts of the Apostles.

'For you will not leave my soul among the dead' — in the netherworld. Yes, indeed: through his death, through his saving death, he has entered into the fullness of the divine-human relationship. He has entered into the reality of sin and refusal.

He redeemed us. He has removed from us the prospect of being ignored by God. Thus this tomb of Jesus hides within its walls all justice tempered by the power of infinite love. Within its walls are hidden the beginnings of the New Life. It is in fact within the tomb that 'God raised him high and gave him the name which is above all other names so that all beings in the heavens, on earth and in the undeworld, should bend the knee at the name of Jesus and that every tongue should acclaim Jesus Christ as Lord, to the glory of God the Father. *(Phil 2:9-11)*

It is in the tomb that death gave way to the resurrection. Through this tomb, redemption has become a hope of life and immortality.

Let us pray,
O Jesus Christ, we all move towards our death, towards our tomb. Grant that in spirit we may pause awhile at your tomb. May the power of life manifested there transfix our hearts. May this life become for us a light on our earthly pilgrimage.

All: Our Father...

> While my body here decays,
> May my soul Thy goodness praise,
> Safe in Paradise with Thee. Amen.

Final Prayer

Let us pray,
Hear, O Father, the plea of your Son who, in creating the new and eternal covenant, became obedient even unto death on the cross; grant that the teachings of his passion may be ever-present in our lives so that we may share in the glory of his resurrection.

He is God who lives and reigns with you in the unity of the Holy Spirit, forever and ever. Amen.